THE
CRIME
WAR

THE CRIME WAR

Robert M. Cipes

THE NEW AMERICAN LIBRARY

THE AUTHOR GRATEFULLY ACKNOWLEDGES PERMISSION TO
REPRINT THE FOLLOWING MATERIAL:

EXCERPTS FROM HERBERT L. PACKER'S REVIEW "THE CHALLENGE OF CRIME
IN A FREE SOCIETY," WHICH APPEARED IN THE OCTOBER 12, 1967, ISSUE
OF THE NEW YORK REVIEW OF BOOKS. © 1967 BY HERBERT L. PACKER.
REPRINTED BY PERMISSION.

AN EXCERPT FROM SIDNEY ZION'S ARTICLE "PROSTITUTION—THE MIDTOWN
ROUNDUP," WHICH APPEARED IN THE NOVEMBER 10, 1967, ISSUE OF THE
NEW YORK TIMES. © 1967 BY THE NEW YORK TIMES CO. REPRINTED BY
PERMISSION.

FIRST PRINTING

PUBLISHED BY THE NEW AMERICAN LIBRARY, INC.
1301 AVENUE OF THE AMERICAS, NEW YORK, NEW YORK 10019
PUBLISHED SIMULTANEOUSLY IN CANADA BY
GENERAL PUBLISHING COMPANY, LTD.
LIBRARY OF CONGRESS CATALOG CARD NUMBER: 68-23036
PRINTED IN THE UNITED STATES OF AMERICA

PORTIONS OF THIS BOOK FIRST APPEARED IN THE ATLANTIC MONTHLY.

For Amy

Acknowledgments

In writing this book I have benefited from many sources. Three of them deserve special acknowledgment. The editors of *The Atlantic Monthly* gave the opportunity for advanced publication of three chapters of the book and contributed to their editorial improvement. My friend Jonathan A. Weiss read the entire manuscript and offered many valuable criticisms and suggestions. Edward T. Chase, Editorial Vice-President of The New American Library, recognized the importance of my subject, lent advice and encouragement at every stage of the writing, and stimulated others' interest in my work. To the extent that the result is worthwhile, he shares in the credit, and regardless of result he has my deep appreciation.

Acknowledgments

Contents

Introduction

"Loose talk about war against crime," said the late Justice Frankfurter, "too easily infuses the administration of justice with the psychology and morals of war." This book is an effort to develop that theme, to show some of the short-range consequences and the long-range dangers of The Crime War. It deals with demagogues who exploit public anxieties about crime and fabricate "crime waves"; with legislators who manufacture enemies by using the criminal law to punish social failures; with prosecutors who seek political advancement by posing as heroes in the war against crime; with police chiefs who compete over who is toughest on crime and who escalate their weapons to meet alleged crises; with a society whose punitive rejection of offenders defeats any chance of rehabilitating them.

This book does not focus on the psychology and morals of the so-called criminal but on the psychology and morals of those who have been set up to prosecute, judge, and punish him. "[I]t is ultimately self-defeating," writes Senator Fullbright, "to 'fight fire with fire,' . . . [Y]ou cannot defend your values in a manner that does violence to those values without destroying the very thing you are trying to defend." The process of waging war, no matter how it is rationalized, nor what rhetoric surrounds it, is a process of moral deterioration. And this holds true for "our" side as well as theirs.

Today there is hysteria about "crime in the streets" and fear of a Negro revolution (which this book shows are closely related). That a ten-percent minority, with far less in power and material resources, could launch a revolution against the rest of America is a fantastic idea, whether it is expressed by white racists or black ones. The real danger of Negro riots is the response they will produce from the forces of "law and order." Robert C. Byrd, a key member of the Senate hierarchy, and former Klan organizer, has advocated that riots be suppressed "with brutal force" and adult looters "shot on the spot." Repression of the riots has already caused more loss of life than the riots themselves. Historically, the worst atrocities have been committed not against but in the name of public security.

Despite popular assumption, individual violence in American life is declining. But not the tendency to collective violence. This tendency is fostered by the moral ambiguities of America's position and by the moral ambiguities in the lives of most Americans. In a world of often unbearable complexity and uncertainty, the thirst for simple solutions is enormous. To most Americans the possession of power is an invitation to use it, not a signal for restraint.

In this climate, the crime war, with its good guys and bad guys, its slogans and scapegoats, fills a need. Information about crime is plentiful and is presented in a way which makes clear the moral dichotomy between society and the criminal. If the dichotomy is false with respect to foreign enemies, it is even falser with respect to domestic enemies. Yet people see what they want to see.

This explains why, at a time when experts have never

had such wide agreement as to reforms necessary, public resistance has rarely been stronger. The public is hardly in a mood to tolerate measures which will teach restraint to policemen, emphasize community relations, or open opportunities for ex-offenders. Measures to "unleash" the police have more appeal, along with laws creating harsher penalties. Only a massive show of force, it seems, will bring release from the social tensions which have been building in this country.

One senses the public mood in following the candidates as they prepare for the 1968 elections. George Wallace gets his loudest applause when he hits at lawlessness and disorder. So does Richard Nixon, whose appeal is even broader. Recently Nixon wrote in *The Reader's Digest*: "In a few short years . . . America has become among the most lawless and violent in the history of free peoples." There has been a "decline in respect for public authority and the rule of law in America." Judicial decisions are "weakening the peace forces as against the criminal forces." Criminals are being turned loose "to prey on an innocent society." There is too much indulgence shown to civil-rights and peace protesters. "Immediate and decisive force must be the first response."

New York Times correspondent Tom Wicker referred to Nixon's article when he predicted that "law and order" will be one of the magic phrases in the 1968 election campaigns. "Politicians will be loudly and endlessly for it. They will view with righteous alarm those who endanger it." But few will talk about what the phrase means. "Which Law and Whose Order?" Wicker asks. The law and order of "a brutal policeman . . . or a landlord whose violations of the sanitary code go unpunished, or politicians who promise everything and deliver nothing?"

America's problem is not really crime, though it may yet

Introduction

become that. The problems are race and poverty. As the Civil Rights Commission has warned, unless solution of these problems is made the nation's first priority, we will continue to be divided—"either torn by violence or coexisting in an uneasy peace purchased at the cost of repressive action."

Santa Barbara
December 1, 1967

THE
CRIME
WAR

I

Crime Waves
and
Crime Commissions

[O]versimplification of the problems of crime and of the criminal law has led the public to expect results that the criminal law machine will never produce, may lead to the uncritical acceptance in the name of crime control of measures that are profoundly unwise and will make it progressively more difficult to direct popular enthusiasm along the most productive channels. . . . [C]rime conference law reform, more successful police, and more capable prosecution cannot cut as deeply into the tough tissues of crime as the public has been led to suppose. . . . [T]he most satisfactory method of crime prevention is the solution of the basic problems of government—the production and distribution of external goods, education and recreation. . . . [O]ne can say for social reform as a means to the end of improved crime control what can also be said for better personnel but cannot be said for drastic tightening of the processes of the criminal law—that even if the end should not be achieved, the means is desirable for its own sake. . . . [T]his should have been the primary message of the crime conferences and the story which the newspapers should have carried.

—Professor Herbert Wechsler (1937)

On March 8, 1965, Lyndon Johnson declared war on crime. Launching the war in a major speech to Congress, the President solemnly warned: *"We must arrest and reverse the trend towards lawlessness. . . .* Our streets must be safe. Our homes and places of business must be secure." It seemed that the President could not have picked a better day to declare war on crime. March 8 was a day on which crime news pushed the Vietnam war to the back pages of the newspapers. The news items ranged from the coercion of a rape confession from George Whitmore, Jr., to the ordering of a jury trial on Jack Ruby's sanity. And in Selma, Alabama, March 8 was a day of high tension after the beating and tear-gassing of civil-rights demonstrators by state police.

"Crime has become a malignant enemy in America's midst," President Johnson's declaration began. Like other political leaders before him, the President sounded as if he had just discovered crime. Yet crime has not "become" a problem. "There has always been too much crime," a report of the President's Crime Commission noted. "Virtually every generation since the founding of the Nation and before has felt itself threatened by the specter of rising crime and violence."

THE CRIME WAR

Four months after he launched the war on crime, the President named the blue-ribbon Commission that would make the most comprehensive survey of crime conditions ever undertaken in this country. The timing of the announcement was dramatic. On the same day, the FBI issued its annual report publicizing the latest crime statistics. In that report FBI Director J. Edgar Hoover made the existence of a crime wave official. Crime in America was growing at a rate six times faster than the population! And while the crime rate was going up, the rate of convictions was going down, a loss which Hoover blamed upon "restrictive court decisions." Though a leading statistical expert stated that Hoover's figures were "not worth the paper they are printed on," the figures made scare headlines, just as they have done since 1930, when Hoover first began to collect and issue crime statistics.

If there is too much crime in America, does it really matter whether the crime rate is high or low compared to other times? Is there any harm in inflating the amount of crime, in claiming a "crime wave" when in fact the crime problem may be not much worse than it has ever been? The answer is yes; comparative rates of crime are important, and there is harm—great harm—in exaggerating the crime problem. If a real emergency exists, the authorities must adopt emergency measures to deal with it. But if in fact there is no crime wave, then there would be no justification in suspending civil liberties, in increasing powers of the police and destructiveness of their weapons, nor any necessity for escalating punishments and tightening security over convicted offenders. The public does need to know the true incidence of crime, the President's Commission concluded; otherwise, it "cannot judge whether the interference with individual liberties which strong crime control measures may involve is a price worth paying."

The Commission's report demolishes the premise that we are in the midst of a crime wave, the very premise, ironically, that gave birth to the Commission. The greatest increase is in crimes which people fear least—crimes against property, such as theft and burglary. Risk from crimes of violence has been exaggerated: "The personal injury that Americans risk daily from sources other than crime is enormously greater." The homicide rate has actually declined over the past thirty years. The risk of death from murder is one out of twenty thousand, about the same as the risk of drowning. The chances of being killed in an accidental fall are twice as great as those of being murdered, and the chances of being killed in a car accident more than four times greater!

The risk of being attacked by a stranger—which is what Americans fear most—is even less than the number of violent crimes indicates. The danger of being assaulted or killed by a relative or acquaintance is actually twice as great. "[T]he closer the relationship," the Commission states, "the greater the hazard. In one sense the greatest threat to anyone is himself, since suicides are more than twice as common as homicides."

How do "crime waves" get started? The Crime Commission found that fears of crime were magnified by lumping statistics for all crimes together and then using violent crimes (the minority) as a stereotype for crime in general. This practice, which the Commission criticized as dangerous, is one which the FBI has been guilty of in its Uniform Crime Reports. "Mass media and overly zealous or opportunistic crime fighters," warns the Commission, "may play a role in raising fears of crime by associating the idea of 'crime' with a few sensational and terrifying

5

criminal acts." Abuse of crime statistics to manufacture a "crime wave" may present more danger to society than crime itself. Says the Commission: "Thoughtless, emotional, or self-serving discussions of crime, especially by those who have the public's attention and can influence the public's thinking, are an immense disservice. They do not and cannot lead to significant action against crime. They can, and sometimes do, lead to panic."

While the Crime Commission lacked sufficient data to say whether Americans today are more or less criminal than Americans in earlier periods, its report reviewed our history of violence to place current conditions in perspective.

A hundred years ago contemporary accounts of San Francisco told of extensive areas where "no decent man was in safety to walk the street after dark; while at all hours, both night and day, his property was jeopardized by incendiarism and burglary." Teenage gangs gave rise to the word "hoodlum"; while in one central New York City area, near Broadway, the police entered "only in pairs, and never unarmed." A noted chronicler of the period declared that "municipal law is a failure . . . we must soon fall back on the law of self preservation." "Alarming" increases in robbery and violent crimes were reported throughout the country prior to the Revolution. And in 1910 one author declared that "crime, especially its more violent forms, and among the young is increasing steadily and is threatening to bankrupt the Nation."

Crime and violence in the past took many forms. During the great railway strike of 1877 hundreds were killed across the country and almost 2 miles of railroad cars and buildings were burned in Pittsburgh in clashes between strikers and company police and the militia. . . . The looting and takeover of New York for 3 days by mobs

6

in the 1863 draft riots rivaled the violence of Watts, while racial disturbances in Atlanta in 1907, in Chicago, Washington, and East St. Louis in 1919, Detroit in 1943 and New York in 1900, 1935 and 1943 marred big city life in the first half of the 20th century. Lynchings took the lives of more than 4,500 persons throughout the country between 1882 and 1930.

The fastest-growing kind of crime today, the Commission reported, was stealing, a crime closely tied to increasing affluence. This trend is shared by all industrialized countries in the postwar period. "Abundance of material goods provides an abundance of motives and opportunities for stealing," particularly for restive urban youth—the postwar generation whose numbers are increasing faster than the rest of our population. Even so, losses to the public from conventional theft are dwarfed by losses from "white-collar" stealing by adults—embezzlement, commercial fraud, tax evasion, antitrust conspiracies. But these crimes do not evoke fear in members of the public.

The Commission's most significant finding is that there is a great deal of *unreported* crime. This does not imply that there is more crime than before, for the phenomenon of unreported crime has obviously existed for some time. It does account, however, for much of the paper increase in crime. With more efficient police work and greater public confidence in the police, more victims are now reporting offenses to the police. Current statistics simply reflect the fact that we are digging more into the reservoir of unreported crime. And this tendency can be expected to continue, producing higher and higher paper increases in the years to come.

Right now the FBI has a virtual monopoly on crime

statistics. Recognizing the many distortions in FBI reports of crimes known to the police, the Commission recommends a national crime-statistics center which would supplement the Bureau's data and try to iron out its distortions. The center would publish statistics and be solely responsible for their interpretation. The real import of the recommendation is that it would deprive J. Edgar Hoover of a weapon which he has used to manipulate public opinion about crime. Hoover has a vested interest in maintaining the crime wave, not only to get ever-increasing appropriations but also to sustain a constant state of emergency in which he can serve as national savior. In my opinion, it is his control of crime statistics, as much as any other factor, which has accounted for his phenomenal dominance of American law enforcement.

That Hoover has been hurt by the Commission's recommendation is obvious from the invective he has used—"the shallow pronouncements of that 'select' group of impractical theorists who would 'define away' and reduce the crime problem by wielding a heavy eraser on [crime] statistics." Yet the Commission treated Hoover delicately in its report, more so than he deserved and more than some of the Commission experts would have liked. For example, in a recent book sociologist Albert Biderman, a key Commission consultant on statistics, attacked the FBI reports for fostering a false image of rapidly increasing lawlessness and for grossly distorting both the rate and distribution of crime. And another Commission consultant, Professor Marvin Wolfgang, detailed in an article the many elements in the FBI reports of "error, omission, inconsistency, contradiction, deficiency, and bias."

Though the Commission denies that a crime wave exists, its report describes a society which is reacting as if it does. Fear of crime has created social costs—in reducing the level of personal contacts, in people staying behind locked doors at night, in unused recreation and other facilities. There is sometimes a poignant note to this, as in the account by Nicholas Katzenbach, chairman of the Commission, of a little old lady whose main pleasure in life was walking her dog. After reading about purse-snatchings and assaults, she became afraid to go out, gave up the walks, and finally had to give the dog away.

Fear of crime, the Commission found, is not associated with actual exposure to crime, either as a victim, a friend of a victim, or a witness. Most people experience crime vicariously, largely through portrayals in the mass media. Several crimes of violence a day in a city of a million people may not mean much statistically, but it can be frightening to the citizen who is bombarded with the gory details every time he picks up his morning newspaper. I think of the spinster who left a good job in Washington and moved to another city because of the "crime wave." Yet the neighborhood she lived in was an exclusive white area with the lowest crime rate in the city.

One of the many myths the Commission shatters is that of interracial crime—of attacks by Negroes on white persons. Commission studies found a minimal amount of such crime. Most Negro crime—like the Negro riots—is confined within the ghetto. Victims of Negro offenders are almost invariably members of the same race. In Chicago, for example, a Negro male risks being a victim of violence nearly six times as often as a white man, a Negro woman nearly eight times as often as a white woman. Almost any crime committed by a Negro against a white makes front-page news, but intraracial Negro murders show up only on the back pages.

The exaggerated fears of personal attack—particularly

9

from the Negro—reflect the enormous amount of ignorance which marks American thinking about crime. But
more than crime, these fears reflect deep anxiety about the
quality of American life. Though the Commission did
not explore the sources of this anxiety, it implies that
attitudes about crime have little to do with actual crime.
The public's fear, it says, is not a simple fear of injury or
death, but "at bottom, a fear of strangers." This is a striking observation. Having made it, however, the Commission
simply drops the subject. Why did it drop it?

The President directed the Commission to find out why
there is a crime wave. But when the Commission's staff
investigated, it found that there was no crime wave, that
the President's premise—and the nation's premise—was
wrong. What was the staff to do? It started out to discover
something about crime and it discovered something else
—a fear of Negroes, a race crisis. But it was not prepared
to deal with the race question. Besides, the subject was
politically explosive; it would have split the Commission
(in which liberals had only a tenuous majority) and
spoiled consensus on other questions directly related to
crime. So the staff left its hypothesis about "fear of
strangers" in the air and left the subject of race itself for
another presidential commission, which would inevitably
have to confront it, as it did in March, 1968.

Yet though the Commission did not deal with white
fears of the Negro, it did deal boldly with the roots of
Negro hostility:

> It is with the young people and the slum dwellers who
> have been embittered by these painful social and eco-
> nomic pressures that the criminal justice system pre-
> ponderantly deals. Society insists that individuals are
> responsible for their actions, and the criminal process

operates on that assumption. However, society has not devised ways for ensuring that all its members have the ability to assume responsibility. It has let too many of them grow up untaught, unmotivated, unwanted. . . . A community's most enduring protection against crime is to right the wrongs and cure the illnesses that tempt men to harm their neighbors.

The Commission rejected the idea that slum riots were "senseless" (an adjective used by J. Edgar Hoover in his 1964 report to the President). It found rather that the riots were deliberate, not in the sense that they were planned, but deliberate in the sense that they were direct attacks on ghetto conditions. "Like any kind of crime," the Commission wrote, "riots are best controlled by prevention. This of course involves maintaining proper police conduct, but the most important element in prevention is a city government's awareness of and response to the frustrations of the community." People who are declared equal by law but are prevented from improving their circumstances, even when they have the ability and desire to do so, "are people with extraordinary strains on their respect for the law and society."

A sociologist describes a slum district in a large city, a ghetto inhabited almost entirely by people of one race:

To the rest of the city it is a mysterious, dangerous, and depressing area . . . [it] is only a few minutes' walk from fashionable High Street, but the High Street inhabitant who takes that walk passes from the familiar to the unknown. For years [it] has been known as a problem area. . . . Respectable people have access to a limited body of information [about it]. They may learn that it is one of the most congested areas in the United States. It

11

is one of the chief points of interest in any tour organized
to show upper-class people the bad housing conditions in
which lower-class people live. Through sightseeing or
statistics one may discover that bathtubs are rare, that
children overrun the narrow and neglected streets, that
the juvenile delinquency rate is high, that crime is preva-
lent among adults, and that a large proportion of the
population was on . . . relief. . . . In this view, people
appear as social work clients, as defendants in criminal
cases, or as undifferentiated members of "the masses."

This was not written as a description of present-day
Harlem or Watts; it is a description of "Cornerville," an
Italian slum which William F. Whyte studied in *Street
Corner Society* thirty years ago. Life in the ghetto has not
changed much—only now its occupants have a different
color.

A generation ago America identified the enemy as Eastern and Southern European immigrants—clinging to alien
ways, yet struggling to break out of the ghetto, to find a
place in the mainstream of America. Granted entry into
the country to provide cheap labor, they began to compete
for jobs with native Americans. Their children overcrowded the schools; their families placed strains on inadequate community services. Unwanted by the majority,
they were stigmatized as immoral, attacked as a threat to
"law and order"—meaning to the dominance of native
Americans.

Politicians in the twenties capitalized on the backlash
and ran on platforms of wiping out crime. Herbert Hoover
was elected President in 1928 on a promise to restore law
and order. It was not until the presidential campaign of
1964, however, that crime control emerged again as a
major domestic issue.

In a time of prosperity the Republicans had to dig deep

for a campaign issue that would arouse the voters without also arousing their anxieties about the candidate, Barry Goldwater. Party strategists saw that their only chance was to exploit the white backlash and the public's distaste for President Johnson's style. Though neither of these themes had much to do with crime, the strategy was to merge them by treating them both as manifestations of crime. In this merger, "crime in the streets" was treated as a product of "crime in high places": use of positions of public power "to feed private greed" set the stage for other forms of lawlessness.

The Republicans hammered away at the Bobby Baker case and at other skeletons in the White House closet, but this did not seem to be paying off. Political corruption rarely can be dramatized in a way that frightens voters. Its effect on the public is too diffuse. The more the appeal of crime in the White House slipped, the more Goldwater pushed the threat of physical violence into the foreground of his campaign:

> Tonight there is violence in our streets. The growing menace in our country tonight, to personal safety, to life, to limb and property, in homes, in churches, on the play- grounds, particularly in our great cities, is the mounting concern or should be of every thoughtful citizen. Security from domestic violence, no less than from foreign aggres- sion is the most elementary and fundamental purpose of any government. . . .

That this appeal was making headway became clear in an opinion poll taken a month before the election. The poll showed a high degree of identity between voters who worried about their personal safety and those who found progress in civil rights "too fast." Goldwater had succeeded in projecting white anxiety about the Negro into fear of Negro criminality. He had tapped latent racist sentiment without having to resort to overt racism. Goldwater's appeal was strong among the lower-middle class—the new suburbanites—many of them children of the immigrants of the twenties. If these people never had it so good, they also never had so much to lose. An article in *Ramparts* described the fear in suburban Cicero:

> There is no telling Jan Vrosak that the black man [across the tracks in Chicago] lives very much like the resident of Cicero, that he may polish his car instead of painting his window sashes but that he too cares about good schools and the safety of the streets and church on Sunday. Jan Vrosak knows better: the black man is poised there waiting to take over, to turn his streets into jungles, to plunge the value of his property. . . . There isn't any white backlash in Chicago. There was never any forward point to lash back *from*.

Johnson won the election despite, not because of, the backlash. In the end the public voted for prosperity; fear that Goldwater might take it away simply proved stronger than fear that Negroes might. But anxiety about crime in the streets and Negroes in the suburbs remained a powerful factor in politics. Though victors in the election, the Democrats were forced on the defensive about crime. For a politician to act "soft" on crime makes him almost as vulnerable as to act soft on Communism. President Johnson had to make some move on the crime front. But what? There is little the federal government can do directly to fight crime. Crime control is essentially a problem of local law enforcement. One way to appear to take immediate action, without seeming to appease the extremists, was to order a survey to determine why there was so much crime and what could be done about it. In March, 1965, just after beginning his new term, the President announced the formation of the Crime Commission.

The backlash sentiment, which Goldwater tried to tap, is as potent in the upper-middle class as in the lower-middle. In both cases the motivation is largely economic. What conservatives are concerned with, as Richard Goodwin has pointed out, is not so much the exercise of authority but its content. A man can oppose the welfare state and at the same time support the police; one is threatening his property rights, the other protecting it. The policeman is his agent. Identity of interest between the citizen and the police may be formalized in the creation of a civic group to support local police. This is the entity known as the citizens' crime commission. It is a permanent action group, as opposed to groups like the President's Crime Commission, which is a temporary study group.

The first citizens' crime commission was established in Chicago in 1919. It was the offspring of the Association of Commerce, whose members were "men of big business affairs." Fighting crime, the Commission said, was good business, for "continuous, preventable crime is just as destructive of property values as a continual series of preventable fires, and the problem of reducing crime is just as much a business proposition as the problem of reducing loss by fire." The Commission newsletter eulogized its founders in these terms: "The word 'failure' was not in their dictionaries. When they undertook a war on crime it meant W-A-R. It also meant that the war would be won."

The tough-minded members of the Chicago Commission complained of "too much meddling by well-meaning people who do not understand crime and criminals." The

Commission's own theories of criminology were simple. Since it considered heredity one of the chief causes of crime, the way to control crime was by sterilization and by eugenics laws, under which all applicants for marriage licenses would have to prove they were morally clean. Another cause of crime was the familiar one—"lack of respect for constituted authority." The Commission worked with the Board of Education and the Committee on Americanism to instill such respect in the city's schoolchildren. Its own brand of Americanism was typified by the slogan: "The United States continues to be a dumping ground for the riff-raff of Europe." Thus the Commission added immigration to its list of causes of crime.

Though the members of the Chicago Crime Commission often sounded like vigilantes, theirs was not the traditional form of frontier justice. They did not believe in taking the law into their own hands, in resorting to violence themselves, but they supported the exercise of violence by the authorities. Commission members were not a lynch mob as such; they simply applauded official hangings and lobbied bitterly against reprieves.

While policemen often complain of a lack of citizen support, sometimes it seems that there is too much support. A cop who enjoys cracking a few heads in suppressing a demonstration should not be encouraged by cheers from the sidelines. As confrontations between police and protest groups increase, police should learn that they have a role which is inconsistent with the needs of vigilantes or with the needs of extremists who want to provoke police brutality for its propaganda value.

There may be a lesson to be learned from the experience of Los Angeles police in Watts. The Chief, the late William H. Parker, believed that all civil-rights activities were "anarchistic" and that any demonstrations were an attempt to defy his authority. After the riot, the Advisory Committee to the U.S. Civil Rights Commission found that for years Parker had been deaf to legitimate complaints of Negro citizens, that the very absence of non-violent outlets in Watts was a cause of the 1965 violence.

Yet it seems that Los Angeles itself may not have learned from the Watts riot. Publisher Otis Chandler of the *Los Angeles Times* (a member of the President's Crime Commission) pointed out that a year after the riot, little had been done to improve the quality of life in Watts. On the other hand, Parker's police had consolidated their power. Parker has become "the white community's saviour," said Chandler, "their symbol of security." Like a true soldier, Chief Parker remained on active duty during the "racial emergency," despite his doctor's advice to retire. Shortly before his death, Parker remarked, "[S]ince Watts, I've never gotten so many awards and citations in my life."

If the police are a symbol of authority to the slum dweller, the symbol has been adopted by other Americans as well, and any threat to the police power is a threat to them. Thus, Chief Parker struck a responsive chord when he said that the police were being limited by the courts "like the Yalu River boundary," and as a result "they are losing the war just like we lost the war in Korea." As Governor Wallace campaigns around the country, he draws his biggest applause when he tells what happens to a molester who attacks a man on the way home from a Wallace rally: "The molester is out of jail before you even get to the hospital. And on Monday morning they try the policeman, and not the criminal!"

The game of blaming the "crime wave" on the courts is not played only by politicians. A "Dick Tracy" comic strip shows a hoodlum assaulting a woman in broad daylight while an audience of onlookers stands by helplessly.

17

As the hoodlum is about to plunge his knife into the victim, he snarls: "Them cowards aren't going to involve themselves and maybe get arrested for violating my constitutional rights."

Not to be outdone by "Dick Tracy," a recent episode of "Little Orphan Annie" has a detective complain to a citizen about how the courts interfere with his job. The detective knows the identity of a gang of hired killers and kidnappers but he can't jail them because "by a recent judicial decision it's illegal for a cop even to ask a suspect his name." But isn't kidnapping a capital offense, the citizen asks in shocked surprise. Sure, the detective replies, "but how long since you've heard of any kidnappers being executed?" Still stunned, the citizen queries: "Isn't there any protection for decent people?"

Propaganda like this creates an image of a persecuted minority, powerless against the tyranny of radical judges and the criminals they protect. The image is false, of course, but the theme it conveys is a familiar one in American politics. Once again a sinister conspiracy is about to envelop all the "decent people," much like the Communist plan to take over the Army and the State Department a decade ago. In fact, this scapegoating of the courts has been appropriately called (by Judge J. Skelly Wright) "The New McCarthyism."

Lately things have gotten so bad for the "decent people" that a group of them, led by conservative lawyers and law enforcement officials, has organized a lobby to file briefs in criminal cases—on behalf of the prosecution! When this supposed minority gets aroused about crime, it can pack a powerful political wallop. In New York City, for instance, middle-class whites—spurred by a scare campaign from the policemen's union—annihilated Mayor Lindsay's civilian review board, and in the 1968 state legislative session they are giving the same treatment to a law restricting the cop's right to kill fleeing suspects.

New York Times reporter Fred Graham has described the parallel between the debate over Vietnam and the controversy over domestic crime control. He describes the "doves," as led by Attorney-General Ramsey Clark (who has shown considerable courage in defending the Crime Commission's recommendations), and the "hawks," as led by Senator McClellan and other conservative members of Congress. McClellan's Subcommittee conducted hearings looking toward overruling the *Miranda* case and later appended a rider to this effect on the Crime Control Act. Southern senators also sought to humiliate Justice Thurgood Marshall, who came before them for confirmation. Discussion of crime control was again used as a cover for racism, as the senators spent most of the sessions pressing Marshall on the police-interrogation question.

The ugly mood of Congress is also reflected in the crime situation in Washington, D.C. Washington was one of the first southern cities to be racially integrated, and southern congressmen—through their control of the District Committees—have worked hard to fulfill their own prophecy that integration cannot work. After ten years of breast-beating about the District's crime wave—and its causal connection with liberal court decisions—southern congressmen finally pushed through an Omnibus Crime Bill for the District. But the bill was unconstitutional on so many grounds that every presidential legal adviser recommended a veto, which is what the President did. This veto was later used by the Republican Policy Committee to blame the President for the 1967 racial disorders. When Congress passed a similar bill in its next session, the President yielded and signed it.

Last year another Presidential Crime Commission,

which dealt with conditions in the District of Columbia, reached the same basic conclusion about crime as the National Commission, namely, that its causes were largely environmental and could be overcome only by massive efforts to upgrade slum conditions. Impatient with this sociological theme and piqued by the President's veto of the tough crime bill, Washington's leading business groups revolted. They organized a Committee to Reduce Crime Now—in other words, a committee which stresses repression and not prevention.

The same emphasis was shown by the House, which quickly passed the incitement-to-riot act but which dallied with the President's Crime Control Act, designed to implement some of the Crime Commission's recommendations. When the Act finally passed the House, its key feature had been emasculated. This would have given the Justice Department control over the type of state program which could qualify for funding and have insured that federal moneys would be spent at least partly on preventive measures stressed by the Commission. While the exact form in which the Crime Control Act will emerge from Congress cannot be known at this writing, legislators have already made clear that first priority will be given to suppression of riots—in other words, to beefing up the police.

This suggests that the careful—in some ways monumental—work of the Crime Commission may prove to have been a waste. Despite attractive packaging, the Commission report has not been widely read outside the professional fields that deal with crime. To the experts, most of the report confirmed what they already knew. It was the politicians and members of the public that the Commission hoped to influence. Apparently the Commission and its staff assumed that the educated answer and scientifically supported conclusion would gain acceptance.

But they overestimated the capacity and receptivity of the politicians and the public. The report stressed that more knowledge is needed to solve the problems of criminal law. Yet the knowledge which the Commission and the experts now have is more than the public can absorb.

There is also a serious question whether the President himself has any real understanding of what the Commission reported to him. If he does, his public statements do not reflect it. He seems unable to break out of the pattern that the 1964 election campaign created, the exclusive preoccupation with crime in the streets, and the premise that America is experiencing a crime wave. Defects of understanding alone make one hesitant to rely on the President's capacity to resist the alarms about crime.

Even before the 1968 campaign is underway, the President's confusion about crime is showing. He tells a Washington audience that "the time has come . . . when the American people are going to rise up and revolt against the lawbreaker in this country," which sounds ominously like advocacy of a fascist takeover. He says that if only crime in the District can be cleaned up, Congress will give the District all the help it needs. But this is the same Congress that passed the vigilante crime bill for the District and now wants to pass one for the rest of the country, the same Congress that obstructed reforms in the District of Columbia police department recommended more than a year before. When the President finally summoned the courage to press for the overdue police reforms, he did so for the wrong reason. He was troubled by FBI statistics which show the District crime rate for October, 1967, to be higher than for the previous October. Yet the District Crime Commission reported that comparisons between single months of different years are notoriously misleading and should not be used. The crime-wave syndrome is by now too firmly implanted in the President's mind to be rooted out.

When conciliatory measures have failed, Fred Graham predicts the President will be under "irresistible pressures to escalate the use of force in the war against crime." Whether or not the President has read the "Report from Iron Mountain"—about the indispensability of public enemies—it appears that the crime war is here to stay.

2

Manufactured Enemies

The common fallacy in thinking about the control of crime is to divorce the question of how to deal with crime from the question of what crime is. . . . [T]he overloading of the criminal justice system . . . can be largely attributed to the burden of investigation, arrest, screening, prosecution, trial and correction of much behavior that has nothing to do with the first concern of a system of public order: the basic security of person and property. Here, as in other aspects of our national policy, appears the fatal American tendency to allow our commitments to outstrip our capabilities.

. . . Our laws against drugs, gambling, and abortions are examples of what may be described as a kind of protective tariff that fosters the activity of the criminal, especially the organized criminal. By outlawing something that people badly want to buy, we increase the seller's risk and therefore drive up the price. . . .

. . . The war between the police and the urban poor probably has been exacerbated by the aggressively interventionist character of our substantive criminal law. Drug use, gambling, and prostitution are a few among the many symptoms of misery whose repression makes the ghetto dweller see the police more as destroyers than as protectors.

THE CRIME WAR

. . . [T]he continued employment of the criminal sanction as the first-line attack of everything we dislike about the behavior of other people represents the height of social [un]wisdom. . . . 'Crime' is an artifact, not a natural phenomenon. Crime is what society chooses to treat as criminal.

—Professor Herbert L. Packer

Several years ago the Attorney General of California conducted an investigation of a gang of motorcycle riders who called themselves the Hell's Angels. A report based on this investigation described the gang's members in frightening terms—as depraved enemies of society who had committed innumerable acts of violence which menaced the peace and order of the state. Now, in a book about the Hell's Angels by Hunter S. Thompson, we are told that the Attorney General's report grossly exaggerated both the size of the gang (one hundred, not four hundred and fifty members) and their offenses, most of which were committed as a result of police harassment or against one another. The ironic result of all this publicity, Thompson writes, was that it rescued the Angels from being disbanded. Inflation of their exploits and of their alleged dangerousness boosted the egos of the members and strengthened their loyalty to the group.

The lesson is that society's attempts to repress delinquency or deviance are usually unsuccessful; too often they succeed only in reinforcing the subculture which produced the delinquent. "At the heart of some of the predicaments in which the criminal law finds itself," says the

Crime Commission, "has been too ready acceptance of the notion that the way to deal with any kind of reprehensible conduct is to make it criminal." After centuries of fruitless search for the causes of crime, many criminologists have come to accept the idea that the major cause of crime is simply the criminal law itself.

Most of the manufactured enemies of society share a common element. As Dr. Karl Menninger has said, they are failures first, criminals second. Thompson's description of the Hell's Angels as "obvious losers"—mostly uneducated and unemployed—bears out this observation. Why, then, does society exaggerate the threat presented by persons like the Angels? Thompson answers: "In a nation of frightened dullards there is a shortage of outlaws." But this is only part of the explanation.

The purpose of criminal law is to maintain order, to protect society and its individual members from acts which threaten its security. But this standard is vague; it must be filled in. What is dangerous cannot be computed on a machine; it involves a human judgment. A citizen is walking late at night on a darkened and empty street; a poorly dressed, unshaven man approaches; he is reeling slightly, maybe the effect of alcohol. Is he a skid-row "bum," merely looking for a handout, or a neighborhood tough who has had one too many and is looking for a fight, or—escalating the possible danger—a vicious mugger, perhaps with a knife or gun? How the citizen reacts will depend on many factors—confidence in his ability to size people up, experience in similar situations, his size and strength compared to the other man's, and his own sense of security or insecurity.

The very concept of "danger" is a subjective one. And just as an individual may lack the power to distinguish between harmful and harmless situations, he may also fail to separate degrees of harmfulness. In an era of mass destruction pollsters continue to find the average American most fearful about "crime in the streets." Given the subjective, often arbitrary, perception of threat, the way in which crime is presented to the public becomes crucial.

History alternates between periods when society is receptive to deviance and periods when it is hostile. Though no one has presented a satisfactory theory to explain this cycle, we can at least identify its ups and downs, the periods of calm and the periods of near hysteria. The latter describes the mood of the late sixties. Frequent alteration in public attitudes toward offenders—from identification to repudiation—means that there cannot be a balanced program of crime control. Polarity in thinking about crime is not of course simply a function of different periods; it also exists during any one period in different elements of the population. Today, for example, experts in criminology are more at odds with politicians as to what should be done about crime control than at any time in recent history. Thus Crime Commission recommendations, like the one favoring rehabilitative treatment in the community for most offenders, rather than prison, are unlikely to be acted upon.

Recently Attorney General Ramsey Clark answered accusations that he was not "tough" enough on crime. In doing so, Clark turned the phony labels of his critics against them: "It is not tough to divert attention from the real problems by criticizing the courts as if they changed human nature or caused crime. Nor is it tough to panic. . . . It requires toughness to recognize many of our jails and prisons for what they are: temporary cell blocks which prepare inmates for further crime."

Unfortunately, Clark's own Department of Justice is not free of polarity about crime control. The chief hawk in the Department is FBI Director Hoover, whom Clark's speech did not name but whose punitive attitude it described. It is Hoover who has propagandized endlessly against "mollycoddling" judges, who boasts of sending convicts to jail last year for a total of forty thousand years, who has demanded stiffer penalties for youthful offenders because the public is "beginning to gag on the steady sociological diet of excusing the conduct of teen-age hoodlums. . . ." Hoover also has the formula for educating youth so that they will have regard for "law and order"—respect for the police officer, religious indoctrination, the Boy Scouts, etc. But this formula for goodness does not always work. In one of Hoover's recent annual reports he featured, as one of the Bureau's most important achievements, the capture of Duane Earl Pope, "convicted of one of the bloodiest bank robberies of modern time." Except for this single aberration, Pope, a deeply religious, hard-working farmboy, could have served as a model for all the qualities which Hoover prizes. Another Hoover model might have been Charles Whitman, the Texas mass murderer—a former altarboy, Eagle Scout, and Marine.

What is to be learned from these unfortunate cases is the danger of creating a dichotomy between good and evil, between the deviant and the rest of society; the danger of assuming moral purity in anyone. Writes psychiatrist Harry A. Wilmer of the "good-guy, bad-guy" myth: "A man may worship at church on Sunday, juggle his income tax returns on Monday, be a scoutmaster on Thursday, and cheat on his golf score on Saturday." In other words, the good guy and the bad guy is in each of us.

Criminologist Donald Taft has said that craving for status and the search for something for nothing—often used to describe the criminal class—are values which are universal in American society. Insurance reports show that millions of dollars' worth of equipment and furnishings are stolen every year from the nation's motels by middle-class guests. This is worth remembering when one reads the shocked accounts of lower-class looting that took place in the 1967 riots. Another sobering fact about relative criminality: the price-fixing violations of twenty-nine electrical-equipment companies, the Crime Commission reported, probably cost the public more money than stolen by burglars in an entire year. "We know that people do not get rich by being good," Clarence Darrow told the inmates of the Cook County Jail, "and that is the reason why so many of you people try to get rich in some other way; only you do not understand how to do it quite as well as the fellow outside."

The prescription and enforcement of the criminal law discriminates sharply against the ordinary offender. The very limitation of his opportunities confines him to crimes which are visible—shoplifting, assaults, auto theft—where the chances of being caught in the act or identified by an eyewitness are greatest. In white-collar crime, on the other hand, proof often depends not on some clear and visible act but on the defendant's state of mind. When he made some claim in order to sell his stock or other product, did he know it was false; did he really intend to deceive? Often it takes an elaborate trial and the verdict of a jury to determine intent. Proof is not a matter of fingerprints or ballistics evidence or items obtained from a search of a defendant's person or premises. Even if he is under suspicion, there is usually no arrest. The prosecutor must convince a grand jury—made up mostly of other white-collar persons—that there was criminal intent.

Perhaps the most important thing about white-collar

29

crime, the Crime Commission concluded, is that the public is indifferent to it, or even sympathetic to the offender who is caught. The Commission quotes an executive sentenced to a short jail term in the electrical conspiracy: "On the bright side for me personally have been the letters and calls from people all over the country, the community, the shops and offices here, expressing confidence in me and support. This demonstration has been a warm and humbling experience for me." "It is unlikely," the Commission adds, "that a convicted burglar would receive such letters and calls."

Upper-class lawbreakers often pose as guardians of public morality against the criminal element. In 1921 Harding's Attorney General, Harry Daugherty, condemned moral decay and lawlessness in a ringing address to the American Bar Association. In 1924, he was forced to resign due to his part in the Teapot conspiracy. In 1933 Richard Whitney, then President of the New York Stock Exchange, wrote an article indicting marginal-stock frauders. Five years later he was indicted himself and sentenced to Sing-Sing for embezzling millions from his brokerage house. Billie Sol Estes, the Texas con man, was an elder of his church, preaching against crime and sin. Censured Senator Thomas Dodd scoured the country for dirty comic books and teen-age subversives as chairman of a Senate Juvenile Delinquency Subcommittee.

The value systems of the upperworld and the underworld are closer than most Americans like to admit. It was Al Capone who said: "The American system gives each and every one of us a great opportunity if we only seize it with both hands and make the most of it." Opportunities for success in established enterprises were closed off to the ambitious immigrant, so the more ruthless ones created their own enterprises. Now the second generation of syndicate men has money to invest, and much of it is going into "legitimate" business. This is supposed to be an insidious and frightening development. That the syndicate's money is dirty money is clear, but we do not trace the source of other money invested in American business. To do so with the syndicate might create a dangerous precedent.

The Crime Commission's report on organized crime is a disappointing rehash of prosecutors' rhetoric. The really sinister aspect of organized crime, it says, is the sermon it preaches: "The government is for sale; lawlessness is the road to wealth; honesty is a pitfall and morality a trap for suckers." The "extraordinary thing about organized crime," the Commission concludes, "is that America has tolerated it for so long." Yet if this is the formula which organized crime has followed, its survival is not extraordinary at all. For it is the same formula which American big business followed in its early stage of development, and in some cases is still following today.

Though the Crime Commission failed to acknowledge it, organized crime is a creature of our puritanical vice laws. It is one of the costs to society of creating a black market in servicing human needs. The process is described in a paper by Commission consultant Thomas Schelling, ignored in the Commission's main report:

> First, it gives the criminal the same kind of protection that a tariff might give a domestic monopoly: it guarantees the absence of competition from people who are unwilling to be criminal, and guarantees an advantage to those whose skill is in evading the law.
>
> Second, it provides a special incentive to corrupt the police, because the police not only may be susceptible to being bought off, but also can be used to eliminate competition.

31

Third, a large number of consumers who are probably not ordinary criminals—the conventioneers who visit houses of prostitution, the housewives who bet on horses, the women who seek abortions—are taught contempt, even enmity, for the law, by being obliged to purchase particular commodities and services from criminals in an illegal transaction.

Fourth, dope addiction may so aggravate poverty for certain desperate people that they are induced to commit crimes or can be urged to commit crimes because the law arranges that the only (or main) source for what they desperately demand will be a criminal source.

Fifth, these big black markets may guarantee enough incentive and enough profit for organized crime so that the large-scale criminal organization comes into being and maintains itself.

Of the millions of arrests made each year, a large percentage are for vagrancy-type offenses. The vagrancy laws are a catch-all for many sorts of behavior. Sometimes they are used as a subterfuge against criminal suspects when there is not enough evidence to hold them on a more serious offense. More often they are used against chronic alcoholics—homeless ones; the middle-class alcoholic is usually taken home by the police or otherwise protected from arrest.

Society's rejection of the vagrant evokes no guilt feelings. The vagrant's filthy clothes and appearance signal that he has sunk to an animal level and justify his being treated as one. If he is sprawled on the sidewalk, no one picks him up, no one looks to see whether in fact he is dead (not an unusual event on skid row). But if a citizen on his lunch hour is bothered too many times by panhandling or by the blight of the vagrant's appearance in a good neighborhood, he sparks a campaign to clean up skid row. Getting the "bums off the streets" can mean a few days in jail or exiling them to some other town, where the process of punishment and banishment is repeated like a revolving door. When the Soviets banish a vagrant, at least they mean business. They send him to penal colonies thousands of miles from civilization.

A clean-up campaign against vagrants is sometimes the answer of the police and courts to the community's demand to get tough on "undesirables" (a favorite euphemism). The criticized officials make a big show of being tough, which is easy when the target is the weakest element in the community. The clean-up campaign may serve a dual function for the police, as both an image-building device and a diversionary tactic, allowing them to go on favoring major crime operators.

Professor Caleb Foote made a revealing study of an anti-vagrancy campaign in Philadelphia, which had been promoted by a "crusading" newspaper. The daily scene in Magistrates Court showed a disreputable-looking and often ill-smelling group, many still shaky from the effects of alcohol. The men were often used for the entertainment of the magistrate, his court personnel, and curiosity-seekers. It was common for the magistrate to address the defendants as "bums" and to treat them with contempt and ridicule. Foote's study debunked the claim that vagrancy laws are an effective harassment device against real criminals. Since the administration of these laws depends on illegality (arrest without cause or charge, for example), the professional criminal can always get a speedy release from jail. Only the paupers and the helpless end up being harassed. Foote concluded that the vagrancy laws are "the garbage pail of the criminal law . . . an easy and convenient dumping-ground for problems that appear to have no other immediate solution."

During the past year the courts have finally begun to rebel against the vagrancy laws. In *Fenster* v. *Leary* the New York Court of Appeals held that state's statute unconstitutional:

> [I]n this era of widespread efforts to motivate and educate the poor toward economic betterment of themselves . . . it is obvious to all that the vagrancy laws have been abandoned by our governmental authorities as a means of "persuading" unemployed poor persons to seek work. . . . It is also obvious that today the only persons arrested and prosecuted as common-law vagrants are alcoholic derelicts and other unfortunates, whose only crime, if any, is against themselves, and whose main offense consists in leaving the environs of skid row and disturbing by their presence the sensibilities of residents of nicer parts of the community, or suspected criminals, with respect to whom the authorities do not have enough evidence to make a proper arrest or secure a conviction on the crime suspected. . . . As to the former, it seems clear that they are more properly objects of the welfare laws and public health programs than of the criminal law and, as to the latter, it should by now be clear to our governmental authorities that the vagrancy laws were never intended to be and may not be used as an administrative short cut to avoid the requirements of constitutional due process in the administration of criminal justice.

More recently the Massachusetts Supreme Judicial Court struck down several vagrancy statutes, explaining that the vagrancy laws were a vestige of the feudal system, aimed at runaway serfs. One of the laws that the court held to be void because of its vagueness subjected to arrest any suspicious person out at night who failed to "give a satisfactory account" of himself. Another law made criminal "idle persons who, not having any visible means of support, live without lawful employment."

Most criminal cases, reports the Crime Commission, "are essentially violations of moral norms or instances of annoying behavior," and not dangerous crimes.

Such behavior is generally considered too serious to be ignored, but its inclusion in the criminal justice system raises questions deserving examination. For one thing the investigation and prosecution of such cases ties up police and clogs courts at the expense of their capacity to deal with more threatening crimes. Moreover, to the extent that these offenses involve willing victims, their detection often requires a kind of enforcement activity that is degrading for the police and raises troublesome legal issues for the courts.

In some cities the enforcement of these laws has been unhappily associated with police, prosecutor, and court venality and corruption, which in turn have led to a general decline in respect for the law. Arrest, conviction, and jail or probation rarely reform persons who engage in these kinds of behavior, nor do they appear to deter potential violators. And continued reliance on criminal treatment for such offenders may blunt the community's efforts to find more appropriate programs to deal with the alcoholic, the homeless man, the compulsive gambler, or the sexual deviant.

No society in the world has been successful in repressing human appetites, but ours continues to persist in the delusion that this is possible. Edwin Schur, a leading authority on "victimless" crime, describes how vice suppression actually reinforces deviance. "[D]eviant self-images and involvement in deviant subcultures are interrelated." Repressive treatment by society drives the outsider

35

further outside, making him even more dependent on others with similar tendencies. The subculture of homosexuality or of drug addiction would clearly be weakened, says Schur, if society were to adopt a more permissive attitude toward deviance. It does not adopt such an attitude because of the deviant's value as a scapegoat. He is "a social sacrifice who complements and at the same time establishes the very possibility of conformity in other group members."

Suppression of vice may often involve an attempt of one group or class to impose its mores on another. This was true of prohibition. One tenet of the prohibitionists was that lower-class criminality was due to alcoholism. Outlaw alcohol and you prevent crime. In fact, prohibition did cut down on petty theft and on the rate of absenteeism among working people. But the era was the most lawless in recent times, not simply because of wholesale violation of prohibition law by affluent citizens but also because of competition among rival syndicates for control of illicit liquor business. We reduced petty crime in order to feed and nurture big crime. The puritanical reformers, who created a black market in the outlawed goods, proved to be the gangsters' chief accomplices.

The pattern of discriminatory enforcement cuts across all vice laws. The organized syndicate with enough business to make police protection a part of its overhead gets immunity. The little man becomes the victim of the clean-up campaign. Society's war against prostitution, like enforcement of other vice laws, usually occurs in a cycle. New York City, for example, has had a "reform" campaign against prostitution about every ten years. Usually the reformers represent members of the business establishment. In 1900, in reaction to a vicious prostitution organization, a Committee of Fifteen was formed by leading citizens. Its revelations shocked the community. Officials responded to public clamor and demanded action; the pressure was passed in typical chain effect down to the front-line troops, the police. The result is described by Judge John M. Murtagh in his book *Cast the First Stone* (co-authored with Sara Harris):

> They got action. Every night plainclothes officers went out into the streets, picked women up by the dozens, and placed them under arrest. They were held along with petty thieves, wife-beaters, and drunks of both sexes. Nobody knew when trial would take place, and the so-called criminals, regardless of whether they would be judged innocent or guilty, had to stay behind bars unless they could muster what came to be known as "the station-house bond." Bondsmen charged phenomenal rates to prostitutes, often twice what they charged others. Since the police were in the habit of bringing the same prostitutes in night after night, it did not take a master mind to recognize the fact that bondsmen and policemen might be in league to fleece the women.

The reformers objected again, and a night court was instituted, where mass-production justice was dispensed. Graft and police brutality flourished. Women with connections got off; others went to jail. But the reformers were dazzled by the unprecedented number of arrests and unconcerned with or unaware of the system's unfairness. "New York would soon become the cleanest city in the country." Judge Murtagh describes how the night court became a rendezvous for fashionable citizens seeking a nighttime diversion after the theater. The court even issued a statement advertising that "there is considerable space for spectators," and "the floor [slopes] from the entrance, so that all have a clear view of the proceedings."

THE CRIME WAR

As a matter of routine, the judges took the word of the vice-squad officers against the women on trial. A young New York lawyer, Anna M. Kross (later New York City commissioner of correction), protested that the kangaroo-court procedures were a travesty on justice. No decent man, she said, would ever take the job of vice-squad plainclothesman. Soon her views were being supported by the new mayor of the city, William Gaynor. A former judge, Gaynor had seen women brought beaten and bleeding into court and knew of entrapment and frame-ups. Once in office, he abolished the vice squad. In a statement of policy which still represents the enlightened—though not the majority—view, Gaynor said: "The business of government is to maintain law, order, and outward decency. Uniformed policemen can doubtless accomplish this business better than decoys can."

Gaynor's regime lasted only three years. At his death, in 1913, the vice squad was restored. Arrests multiplied, and the reformers were pleased with the seeming cleanliness of the city. In 1917 the Bureau of Social Hygiene, one of the Rockefellers' early philanthropic efforts, boasted that vice in New York had been brought under control by the police. From the number of women dragged into court, however, one would never know it. Anna Kross continued to raise a dissenting voice, protesting that prostitution had not been checked at all, that police activity had simply driven the underworld to resort to more secretive methods and created more need for graft. "The rounding up and incarcerating of unfortunate prostitutes does not solve the problem."

In the early thirties new scandals rocked the Women's Court, unearthed by the zealous investigation of Judge Samuel Seabury (the man responsible for Jimmy Walker's downfall). Seabury uncovered a vicious ring of extortionists, most of whose members were public officials. One of them was the darling of the reformers throughout the twenties, Assistant District Attorney John C. Weston. Weston, it turned out, had pocketed at least twenty thousand dollars in graft during this period by going easy on defendants. The game the ring played was not bribery so much as shakedown. They did not take money to kill an existing prosecution but usually created the prosecution for the very purpose of the payoff.

A colorful side of the ring was its use of an agent provocateur with the name of Chile Mapocha Acuna. Acuna's testimony put the finger on the public officers who were his partners. Their strategy began by placing their female victim in a compromising situation. Often the victims were prostitutes to begin with, but sometimes they were not. A favorite routine used on innocent women was "the doctor's-office caper." Acuna would enter a doctor's office and in the presence of the nurse begin disrobing. At that moment the vice-squad officers would burst in and "raid" the premises, finding the dollar bills which Chile had carefully planted in the room. Later, in jail, the terrified nurse would be visited by a go-between, typically one of the corrupt bail bondsmen who flourished during the period. He would tell her that for the right price he could steer her to a lawyer who would fix the case so she would not get a prison sentence. Five hundred was an average price, but if the victim had more, unexpected "complications" would arise requiring additional payments. After the arrest, Chile, the agent who provoked the incident, would disappear. The scheme was conveniently designed so that his testimony was not crucial, since the vice-squad officers themselves had witnessed the incriminating scene.

The ring was so successful that in a few years five of the officers had accumulated a total of one-half million dollars.

Only a year after the Seabury report, the number of arrests began to climb again. The main target became Negro streetwalkers. Again it was necessary for Anna Kross to dissent, as she had done twenty-five years before. Now, however, she spoke with new authority; in the interim, she had become a magistrate herself: "We are proceeding through this court against the victims of prostitution rather than against the structure of commercialized vice. We see here the bankrupts of their profession . . . the friendless, the girls and women who are so unsuccessful even at this profession that they have no regular clientele but must solicit their business on the streets." Women whose profession had brought them riches, and their procurers, were not seen in the Women's Court.

Thirty years later, Judge Kross's words are being echoed in New York. In September 1967 the state's penal revision took effect, reducing the maximum penalty for prostitution from one year to fifteen days, overdue recognition that the law has been enforced against the failures and not the successful prostitutes. At first it was reported that Commissioner Howard Leary was ordering his men to cease making arrests, in the belief that his force was being demoralized by the corrupt practices inevitably fostered by prostitution enforcement. But then began what Sidney Zion called the "Greatest Dragnet of All Time." Describing a three-month period during which twenty-four hundred arrests were made, Zion wrote in *The New York Times:*

> . . . [T]he action was carried out with astonishing ease, made possible by the combination of silence and a

subtle double-play on the Constitution—making arrests on vague and indefinite grounds, which is a violation of due process, and on suspicion without probable cause, which contravenes the Fourth Amendment, and then dismissing the charges without trial.

What happened was that the police, upset by complaints of midtown businessmen and reportedly under pressure from City Hall to halt an apparent rise in street-walking, decided to pick up the girls en masse by means of the state's disorderly conduct statute. . . . "It's un-profitable and un-economic to make solicitation arrests," Deputy Commissioner Jacques Nevard explained. . . . "We're trying to sweep the streets so that people can walk without being assaulted by these brazen women, and it's more effective to arrest them for disorderly con-duct."

The trouble is that it's about as constitutional as a mugging, a fact tacitly conceded by the district attorney's office which invariably moved to dismiss the disorderly conduct charges. . . . But dismissals did not hamper the "street-sweeping" purpose of the dragnet. The cops would pick the girls up at midnight or thereabouts, place them in cells and not be required to bring them to court until the morning. . . . So in any event the girls arrested were out of business for the night and could always be arrested again the following evening.

When the police found out that a test case was going to be made of the practice, they switched the basis for the arrests to loitering, a variety of the vagrancy laws. But finally a test was made of the loitering arrests, and they were declared illegal by the Criminal Court. New York's Finest had to turn to hunting down other public enemies.

A familiar image shows the law enforcer as a forgotten soldier in the front lines, fighting against a dirty enemy, while the public back home refuses to give him the weapons he needs for victory. Recently *Life* magazine glorified the Detective, fighting the war of the Times Square jungle. "I've got to win," the Detective says, "and these animals can smell it."

But who are these animals? The Detective says his mission is to wipe out the "bad guys," whom he defines as professionals who pursue crime as a brutal way of life. But how many of those he comes in contact with meet that definition? His own statistics show that most crimes reported in his precinct, aside from prostitution, are larcenies (from pickpocketing to shoplifting). There are relatively few robberies and about as few "felonious assaults," most of them fights involving no dangerous weapon. The "animals" with whom the Detective is at war, then, turn out to be mostly petty thieves, prostitutes, junkies, and homosexuals—the least dangerous of the "criminal" population.

Repression of homosexual activities is more severe than of illegal heterosexual activities. Occasionally the punishment imposed on homosexuals is grotesque. Recently in Yemen a convicted homosexual was executed for the crime before a mob of six thousand. Harry Golden reports a thirty-year sentence in North Carolina in a case of consenting adult homosexuality. These sanctions are unusual, however; the common evil is threat of exposure, which makes homosexuals the prey of vice-squad shakedowns as well as of private extortionists.

Since enforcement of homosexual laws is intermittent, it is often fair to look for some private motive when a homosexual is prosecuted. This is suggested by a recent book about a scandal in Boise, Idaho, where the conservative business community, ostensibly to stimulate political reform, exposed a homosexual group that had existed for some time with the knowledge of the police. In the demand for retribution that followed the exposure, the members of the group convicted received long prison terms. One of them was sentenced to life.

In Washington, D.C., police have finally abandoned the practice of peeping into men's rooms to discover homosexual activities. This particular reform may be related to the unfortunate case of Walter Jenkins. Just before the 1964 election, President Johnson's closest adviser was arrested for engaging in homosexual activities in a restroom at a Washington YMCA. News of the arrest was leaked for political purposes. The publicity ended Jenkins' public career, apparently a useful one; worse than that, it destroyed his personal reputation. But instead of causing a wave of revulsion against vice-squad peeping, the Jenkins case caused public shock about possible "security" violations. J. Edgar Hoover had to prepare a special report to reassure the public that there was no violation of security. Last year Ronald Reagan, one of those who tried to capitalize on Jenkins' misfortune, had his own homosexual scandal. Though there was a certain poetic justice in Reagan's predicament, Drew Pearson's creation of the scandal was a dirty trick: a politician is damned if he admits he employed homosexuals and damned if he denies it. And in this case—involving state and not federal government—"security" is not even available as an excuse for exposure. But politics needs footballs, and the homosexual seems as good a one to kick around as any.

Despite the professed aim of vice laws to eliminate deviant behavior, the result has been to create black markets in which appetites continue to be fed—but at an awful price. Concludes Edwin Schur in *Crimes Without Victims:*

Despite pious protestations, it seems clear that the repressive policies . . . represent societal decisions as to how the various demanded goods and services are to be allocated. Embodied in these decisions is an insistence that social approval shall not attach to the transactions in question; but also implied is the recognition that the particular goods and services shall in one way or another be made available. . . . The drug addict is to obtain his drugs, but not from legitimate medical sources. The homosexual is to pursue his sexual inclinations, but must conceal his condition and submit to a certain amount of segregation. Of course very few citizens in our society would express the collective decisions in this way. Yet one is forced to conclude that for one reason or another it has been "arranged" that these social problems shall remain insoluble.

Looked at another way, it may not pay to change the arrangement. We would only manufacture other enemies to take the place of these.

3

The Meanings
of
Miranda

[I]t has been my observation that by far the greater
number of law enforcement officers are honest and sin-
cere in their desire to enforce the law, and that they
will gladly submit to the supervision of any duly constituted authority that will assist them in the performance
of their duties.

—District Attorney Earl Warren (1934)

3

The Meanings of Miranda

M̲ore than thirty years ago, when Earl Warren was a career district attorney in California, he came to Washington to address a national conference on crime. His approach to crime control was dispassionate and objective. Distrustful of panaceas, he saw that the basic needs of law enforcement were improving its administration and personnel. He rejected vigilante groups whose solution to crime was enacting harsher penalties and giving more procedural advantages to the state. This he called a "popular war cry."

District Attorney Warren's speech paid tribute to the director of the Federal Bureau of Investigation, J. Edgar Hoover, for helping the states elevate their standards of law enforcement. Yet when Hoover spoke at the same conference, he sounded the "war cry." We are facing "desperate men and equally desperate women," he warned, "who have respect only for a power greater than theirs." The criminal "rules by fear, and fear is the only weapon which can rule him—fear of the certainty of arrest and punishment." He boasted of his ninety-four-percent conviction record and promised that the Bureau would continue "to pursue relentlessly and prosecute fully—and to fearlessly meet the challenge of the underworld even though it means a war to the death."

That men of such divergent philosophies as Warren and Hoover could find a common meeting ground in 1934 is unusual, but it is less unusual than their finding a common ground once Warren became Chief Justice of the Supreme Court. Yet when Warren delivered his opinion in the case of *Miranda* v. *Arizona* on June 13, 1966, J. Edgar Hoover emerged as a champion of civil liberties and the FBI as a model for police-interrogation practices. This is only one of the ironies of the *Miranda* decision, which affects the balance of power between the police and the accused at a time when most of the nation, like Hoover, sees itself engaged in a life-and-death struggle against crime.

In reversing the convictions of four men because of improperly obtained confessions, the Court made new rules for police interrogation. It said that no statement of a suspect may be used to convict him unless his privilege against self-incrimination has been scrupulously protected. *Miranda* was decided almost two years to the day after the Court's opinion in *Escobedo* v. *Illinois*. There the Court reversed a murder conviction because the suspect confessed after being denied access to his lawyer. *Escobedo* left open the question whether indigent suspects— some two-thirds of those arrested—were entitled to similar protection. This question was answered affirmatively in *Miranda*.

Since *Escobedo*, the Warren Court has been a whipping boy of police, prosecutors, and their supporters. Some police officials—like Chicago's O. W. Wilson, to whose men Escobedo confessed—flatly instructed their officers to ignore the decision. Wilson claimed that the opinion was confusing, and he challenged the Court to issue clear guidelines for the police. In *Miranda*, the Court accepted the challenge, setting down a detailed code of interrogation procedures.

The essential elements of the code are these: As a general rule the state may not use statements resulting from "custodial interrogation" unless the police observe safeguards against self-incrimination. "Custodial interrogation" goes beyond station-house detention. It applies whenever the police deprive a suspect "of his freedom of action in any way." The following are the minimum safeguards required:

1. A warning that the suspect has a right to remain silent and that any statements made may be used as evidence against him.

2. Advice that he is entitled to consult a lawyer prior to interrogation, and that if he cannot afford a lawyer, the state will make one available to him.

3. If a suspect rests on his privilege, or states he wants a lawyer, the police must discontinue questioning. This is true at any stage of the interrogation.

4. If the suspect wants and gets a lawyer, questioning may continue, but it must be in the presence of the lawyer.

5. The privilege against self-incrimination and the right to counsel may be waived, if the waiver is made voluntarily. But the "heavy burden" of proving a waiver is on the state.

Despite this detailed code, which goes beyond the issues presented in the four cases, and despite the sharp dissents of four justices, the Court's opinion in *Miranda* is essentially a logical outgrowth of *Escobedo*. Its significance lies not so much in breaking new legal ground as in bringing into focus some critical social problems.

The *Miranda* case has many meanings. It reflects a deep dichotomy of opinion as to crime control. Can we deal adequately with the crime problem without sacrificing some of our civil liberties? What does *Miranda* mean to the ability of the police to solve crimes? Are confessions indispensable, and will the rules set down by the Court eliminate confessions? If police officers cannot comply with the new rules without sacrificing confessions, will they create techniques for evading the rules? At the ethical level, *Miranda* challenges the propriety of the means used by society to catch and punish those who deviate. The final meaning of *Miranda* is its reflection of a growing polarity in American values—between authority and conformity on the one hand and liberty and dissent on the other.

Until the *Escobedo* decision, state police and prosecutors had little cause to criticize the Supreme Court's confession cases. The Court exercised only a narrow review over state-police methods. To reach the Court, a state defendant had to show some violation of due process, usually the use of the third degree—which means physical or psychological coercion. Police smarted for a time under the Court's search-and-seizure rules, but they seemed to be able to live with them.

On some other issues there was even a mild consensus among the courts and the police. One such issue was reforming the bail system to remove financial discrimination. Another was ensuring free trial counsel for the indigent, reflected in the Supreme Court's unanimous opinion in *Gideon* v. *Wainwright*. In May of 1964 the Justice Department sponsored a National Conference on Bail. At the opening session Chief Justice Warren shared the platform with Police Commissioner Michael Murphy of New York. The Chief Justice told Murphy he was "inspired and heartened" by the Commissioner's support of a project to eliminate the stigma of arrest in minor offenses. And Murphy spoke earnestly of his department's efforts in "furthering the individual rights and liberties of the accused."

The truce between the police and the defense-oriented justices was an uneasy one, however, though few persons imagined the break would come as soon as it did. Only a year after the bail meeting, Warren and Murphy again appeared together, this time at a judicial conference in Atlantic City. In the interim Murphy had resigned his job in resistance to demands for creation of a civilian review board, the Warren Court had decided the *Escobedo* case, and Barry Goldwater had made "crime in the streets" a major political issue. This time Murphy wasted no breath on amenities nor on homage to civil liberties. Reflecting the change in public mood, he excoriated the Warren Court for hampering law enforcement while "vicious beasts" were loose on the streets. He protested that police were being forced to fight by the Marquis of Queensberry rules, "while the criminals are permitted to gouge and bite."

Murphy's rhetoric was a familiar part of the battle imagery which permeates law enforcement. President Johnson in his 1966 crime message, for example, referred to the local policeman as "the front-line soldier in the war on crime." Comparing the police to front-line soldiers evokes a demand for more weapons. Thus, in lobbying for a stop-and-frisk law, New York district attorneys made this appeal: "In every war America has always equipped its armies with the best and most modern weapons. We in law enforcement are engaged in a continuous war in peacetime. We ask only that we be properly equipped to meet the criminal enemy and to make certain that law enforcement and the public are not left defenseless in the war against crime."

51

The cry that the police were being handcuffed was a familiar one in at least one American city—Washington, D.C. In 1957 the Supreme Court in the *Mallory* case set aside a rape confession (and death sentence) because the police had unreasonably delayed in taking the nineteen-year-old Negro defendant before a magistrate. The confession was excluded not on constitutional grounds but under the Court's power to maintain civilized standards of federal law enforcement. The Court refused to inquire whether the confession was voluntary or involuntary, reliable or unreliable. It recognized that when police hold a man incommunicado there is a temptation for questioning to slide into the third degree and the added temptation for the questioner later to testify falsely about the circumstances of the confession.

Law-enforcement officers in the District and their friends in Congress were particularly exercised because the *Mallory* rule operated in favor of the guilty. Mallory himself represented not just the escape of a guilty man, but the return of a dangerous criminal to the community. After his release he committed rape in another city. Statistics compiled by the District Crime Commission show that only a small fraction of criminal convictions are reversed on *Mallory* grounds, and that only a few of the beneficiaries escape punishment entirely. But sobering facts such as these have a way of escaping notice in a community aroused by "crime waves."

For ten years House and Senate committees which control the District worked for a law to overrule the *Mallory* case. Bills were proposed and lengthy hearings held. The cast of characters at each hearing was generally the same. One commuter to Capitol Hill was District of Columbia Police Chief Robert Murray; the *Washington Post* accused him of spending so much energy lobbying against the *Mallory* rule that he had neglected his real job. Chief Murray's stock theory was that the rule actually caused an increase in crime, because "sharp, shrewd and calculating criminals" from other states were coming to the District in order to commit crimes with immunity. Murray's successor, Chief John Layton, took a more reasonable tack, claiming *Mallory* influenced not the rate of crime but the rate of *clearance* of crime. This year Congress finally overruled *Mallory* in the D.C. Omnibus Crime Bill. Flushed with success, it is preparing the same treatment for *Miranda*.

No person "shall be compelled in any criminal case to be a witness against himself." This Fifth Amendment privilege against self-incrimination is the focus of the *Miranda* opinion. The privilege has long been applied to protect an accused at his trial. *Miranda* makes clear that the privilege gives the same protection to a suspect under police interrogation.

The privilege stemmed from abhorrence with the Star Chamber statute of 1487 in Tudor England, under which a defendant could be forced to testify at his trial in order to elicit a confession. The proceedings had a familiar justification, that "little or nothing may be found" by other means of investigation. The constitutional protection against the use of coerced confessions—the due-process rule—had a different origin. Until the 1600's in England it was common to extract a confession by means of torture. Such confessions were by their very nature unreliable, which was not necessarily true of confessions obtained in violation of the privilege. Until *Miranda* the two types of confessions had generally been treated separately. In *Miranda* the distinction is blurred, for the Court seems to suggest that police interrogation is inherently coercive.

53

To the majority of the Court, the most dangerous aspect of such interrogation is that it takes place in secret in a police-dominated atmosphere. The "very fact of custodial interrogation exacts a heavy toll on individual liberty and trades on the weaknesses of individuals." In the *Escobedo* case Justice White's dissent complained that the majority opinion reflected "a deep-seated distrust of law enforcement officers everywhere, unsupported by relevant data or current material based upon our own experience." Conscious of this complaint, the Chief Justice in *Miranda* marshals current facts about coerced confessions, such as the sixty-one-page false murder confession in the *Whitmore* case, and the case of the Brooklyn police burning an uncooperative witness with lighted cigarettes. The Chief Justice also refers to Civil Rights Commission reports of police brutality in the South.

But the principal evidence of coercion set forth in the opinion is not physical but psychological. The Court quotes at length from interrogation manuals authored by the top criminal-detection experts in the country—widely used by the police, as evidenced by sales of forty-four thousand copies. These manuals represent the "modern, scientific" approach to police interrogation—methods developed after the third degree had been discredited. The leading manual cited in *Miranda* is *Criminal Interrogation and Confessions,* coauthored by Professor Fred Inbau of Northwestern University, long a critic of the *Mallory* rule and the favorite witness of congressional committees seeking to overrule *Mallory*. It was Inbau who told Congress in 1963 that sanctions against the police were no longer necessary because the old third degree had been replaced by psychological interrogation. It was Inbau also who was indirectly responsible for the *Escobedo* case. The Chicago police, whom Inbau advises, got Danny Escobedo to confess by using the trick Inbau calls "playing one against the other." The police let Danny think that he would have to take the rap for his accomplice, who had actually pulled the trigger.

A reading of Inbau's book gives an illuminating insight into the "scientific" method. First, a description of the interrogation room: There are no windows. In a police station, windows must contain bars, and this naturally would discourage a confession. There are no distracting objects in the room, no telephone, no ashtrays (indicating there is no smoking). The chairs have straight backs to discourage relaxation. The interrogator takes no notes, is completely absorbed in the subject, and gives the impression of having unlimited time for questioning. The following are examples of Inbau's suggested "Tactics and Techniques for the Interrogation of Suspects Whose Guilt Is Definite or Reasonably Certain":

"Sympathize with the subject by telling him that anyone else under similar conditions or circumstances might have done the same thing." In a wife-killing case, where investigation shows the husband has been treated "very miserably over the years," this line of examination is suggested:

"Joe, as recently as just last week my wife had me so angry with her nagging that I felt I couldn't stand it any more, but just as she was at her worst the doorbell rang and we had some out-of-town company. Was I glad they came! Otherwise I don't know what I would have done."

"Reduce the subject's guilt feelings by minimizing the moral seriousness of his offense." In getting Danny Escobedo to talk, the Chicago police let him think he was less culpable than his accomplice, though under the law he could be punished just as severely. In questioning a thief, Inbau recommends showing the suspect one of Inbau's own articles. This says that "about 85 of every 100 persons will 'steal' if the opportunity to do so is presented to them." The guilt-reducing technique is not only effective in getting confessions; apparently it can also be therapeutic. A few days before being executed, one subject told Inbau how comforted he had been by Inbau's statement—just prior to confessing—that this crime was actually "no worse" than any of his others.

A favorite technique of interrogators is the friendly-unfriendly, or "Mutt-and-Jeff," act. The *Miranda* opinion quotes from one of the police manuals:

> . . . In this technique, two agents are employed, Mutt, the relentless investigator, who knows the subject is guilty and is not going to waste any time. He's sent a dozen men away for the full term. Jeff, on the other hand, is obviously a kindhearted man. He has a family himself. He has a brother who was involved in a little scrape like this. He disapproves of Mutt and his tactics and will arrange to get him off the case if the subject will cooperate. He can't hold Mutt off for very long. The subject would be wise to make a quick decision. The technique is applied by having both investigators present while Mutt acts out his role. Jeff may stand by quietly and demur at some of Mutt's tactics. When Jeff makes his plea for cooperation, Mutt is not present in the room.

In cataloging the evils of the coerced confessions, the Court referred to the Wickersham report on "Lawlessness in Law Enforcement." Issued in the early thirties, this report of a presidential commission shocked the country with its revelations of third-degree practices and had some influence on police officials to clean house. The Wickersham Commission found that the third degree actually impeded rather than aided crime control: "[It] brutalizes the police, hardens the prisoner against society, and lowers the esteem in which the administration of justice is held by the public."

The Wickersham report also reviews the arguments made in defense of the third degree. Many of them are still made today, but one has a distinctly original flavor. Referring to the necessity of the third degree in controlling crime, a police chief complained that his department was being discriminated against: "A policeman should be as free as a fireman to protect his community. Nobody ever thinks of hedging a fireman about with a lot of laws that favor the fire."

"Were we to limit these constitutional rights to those who can retain an attorney," the Chief Justice wrote, "our decisions today would be of little significance." He pointed out that each of the four cases, like the vast majority of confession cases, dealt with defendants unable to retain counsel. "While authorities are not required to relieve the accused of his poverty, they have an obligation not to take advantage of indigence in the administration of justice."

The Court thus rejected the position of Attorney General Katzenbach and his chief adviser on criminal procedure, Harvard Professor James Vorenberg. In writing the proposed Model Code of the American Law Institute, Vorenberg and his fellow draftsman had stated: "Criminal justice is not a sport or game, and notions of fairness derived from the moral structure of games, premised on legitimation of self-interests to the fullest extent consistent with the game, are by no means persuasive." In defending Vorenberg's draft, Katzenbach said the same thing in more colloquial terms: "I have never understood why the gangster should be made the model and all others raised in the name of equality, to his level of success in

57

suppressing evidence. This is simply the proposition that if some can beat the rap, all must beat the rap."

A month before the *Miranda* opinion was issued, the Law Institute met in the shadow of the Supreme Court to discuss the Model Code draft. A spokesman for the Institute's liberal wing, Federal Circuit Judge George Edwards, accused the draftsmen of pressuring the Court in the hope of narrowing the scope of the pending decision. It was rumored, on the other hand, that the decision had already been written and that the justices had made a tactical decision not to release it prior to the ALI meeting. Chief Justice Warren, who addressed the meeting and stayed to hear part of the debate on interrogation, gave no clue as to the truth of the rumor. After two days of often bitter discussion, the liberal wing seemed to be vindicated, with Vorenberg and his staff expressing willingness to return to "the drawing board." Had *Miranda* been issued prior to the ALI meeting, thus preempting debate, the Court might have been accused of disregarding the opinions of this prestigious body. As it turned out, the debate showed the difficulty of reaching a clear consensus while rejecting the Vorenberg-Katzenbach approach, and thus created a favorable climate for the direction which the Court was to take in *Miranda*.

In his *Escobedo* dissent, Justice Byron White anticipated that the Court would soon require appointment of counsel prior to interrogation. This rule, he said, would be "wholly unworkable and impossible to administer unless police cars are equipped with public defenders." Chief Justice Warren probably had this in mind when he disclaimed that *Miranda* required each police station to have a "station-house lawyer." But if the police want to interrogate, the only alternative to a station-house lawyer is waiver of a lawyer—something which the *Miranda* rules theoretically are loaded against.

Does the presence of a lawyer mean an end to questioning? The opinion says that "an attorney may advise his client not to talk to the police until he has had an opportunity to investigate the case." The statement would be more accurate if "must" were substituted for "may." Since an attorney is sworn to protect his client's rights, he risks violating his oath by turning the client over to the police before he knows all the facts. Only when the client is actually innocent or has a solid defense (like self-defense) will it benefit him to talk to the police.

That an attorney advises his client not to talk, said the opinion, is no cause for considering him "a menace to law enforcement." As Justice Jackson once stated, the criminal lawyer has no duty to help society solve its crime problem. It is true that defense counsel usually end up advising clients to plead guilty. But this is a tactical decision based on many factors, after the lawyer has discovered something of the state's evidence and had a chance to bargain with the prosecutor. It is very different from surrendering at the outset.

In the adversary trial the defense lawyer contributes to the appearance of due process. Convicting an accused without giving him counsel is such a visible inequity that even authoritarians reject it. Though the lawyer occasionally obstructs enforcement by defeating conviction, his essential role is to keep the wheels of the prosecution machinery turning. The conscience of the community is eased by the belief that no man is unjustly convicted.

The role of the lawyer at the investigatory stage, however, is more than ceremonial. Nothing could better illustrate the difference than the Court's vote in the *Gideon* and *Miranda* cases. In *Gideon*, guaranteeing trial counsel, the justices were unanimous; in *Miranda* they split five to four. Because police investigation is normally shielded from public scrutiny, the entry of defense counsel is a nuisance. Putting counsel in the police station tests the framework of the adversary system—a system which boasts of being "accusatorial," while permitting inquisitions to flourish invisibly in back rooms. Recognizing the hypocrisy of this position, the Court in *Miranda* attempts to make the criminal process conform to its image. In doing so, however, it inevitably casts the lawyer in an obstructive role.

To soften this impact, *Miranda* tries to minimize the role of the lawyer. In *Escobedo* the Court had been accused of obscuring the self-incrimination issue by pitching the decision on access to a lawyer. Now the Court changes field and reverses the relative importance of the two rights. *Escobedo* is a "right-to-counsel" case, *Miranda* a "self-incrimination" case. But if *Escobedo* obscured the underlying problem of self-incrimination, *Miranda* obscures the practical effect of counsel on interrogation. For the majority to suggest that the lawyer might help the police was, as Justice Harlan said, "fanciful." But to confess that the lawyer would probably put an end to questioning would have required the majority to acknowledge the meaning of *Miranda*. The Court was not prepared to announce to a crime-anxious society that the elimination of confessions is the inevitable direction in which it is moving.

To require the police to protect the suspect's self-incrimination privilege by warnings and other safeguards is one thing; to enforce the requirements is another. Professor Vorenberg was skeptical that *Miranda* would affect existing practices. The opinion "just moves the battleground from the voluntariness of the confession back to the voluntariness of the waiver" of defendant's rights. The courts still have to decide on a case-by-case basis whether the police or the defendant is telling the truth about waiver. And, Vorenberg added, "the police have done pretty well with these swearing contests over the years."

The *Miranda* opinion seeks to avoid the swearing contest by putting a "heavy burden" on the state to prove effective warnings and a voluntary waiver. But it does not suggest what type of proof would be appropriate. Vorenberg's ALI Code draft, for example, provided for sound recordings of interrogations or the presence of a neutral observer at the police station. In leaving the methods of proof entirely open, the Court invited litigation on this issue. Lower courts, more in sympathy with the goals of the police, are likely to accept less proof than the Court would, and eventually the problem may have to come back to the Court for resolution.

In trying to show that law enforcement would not be impeded by the new rules, the Court reached out for precedents from other countries. Its selection of England as a model was unfortunate, for the English Judges' Rules are far less rigid than *Miranda*. To rely on their example is to suggest that *Miranda* will be evaded and watered down in practice. The English rules require advice to a suspect about silence but not the right to an attorney. The suspect may retain counsel, but counsel can be excluded if the police find he would interfere with their investigation. Even if the rules are violated, the judge may permit the confession to be used, something forbidden by our automatic exclusion. The English judge may also comment to the jury on the defendant's silence when questioned, a comment which would violate our Fifth Amendment. Finally, even when a confession is not allowed in court, the English police may still use other evidence discovered as a result of that confession.

That English practice was a poor example to choose was underlined a year after *Miranda* was decided. A leading English legal group issued a report proposing compulsory interrogation of all criminal suspects. Six years before, the same group had rejected a similar proposal as "alien to the general conception of justice in this country." Now it explained that "the climate of opinion has become less favourable to criminals," evidence that the crime war is not strictly an American phenomenon.

Another technique used by the Chief Justice to evoke support for *Miranda* was to identify the decision with the Federal Bureau of Investigation. If the Court could suggest that its rules were not new but simply a copy of what the Bureau had been doing all along, it could head off a lot of criticism. "Over the years," the Chief Justice wrote, "the Federal Bureau of Investigation has compiled an exemplary record of effective law enforcement," despite its warnings to suspects about the privilege against self-incrimination and right to counsel. What the Chief Justice did not make clear is that the FBI warning omitted the crucial element required by *Miranda*—that the indigent suspect has the right to appointed counsel prior to interrogation.

In hiding behind the FBI image, the opinion was disingenuous enough, but the Chief Justice went even further and quoted from a J. Edgar Hoover law-review article on civil liberties: "Law enforcement, however, in defeating the criminal, must maintain inviolate the historic liberties of the individual. To turn back the criminal, yet, by so doing, destroy the dignity of the individual, would be a hollow victory."

It sounded like Hoover had come a long way since 1920. Then, as chief of the Bureau's General Intelligence Division, he was instrumental in the dragnet arrests of thousands of aliens whom the government wished to deport as subversive. At that time Hoover felt it was vital to secure confessions of radicalism from the prisoners. A federal judge found that the aliens were "frightened by the terroristic methods of their arrest and detention." Hoover denied that any force was used, but instructions to his agents stressed the value of midnight arrests and the necessity of holding prisoners incommunicado until they confessed. Writes Max Lowenthal in his classic history of the FBI:

> Mr. Hoover thought it was dangerous to let the prisoners have a lawyer present, or to let them talk with a lawyer or to communicate with one in any way, until after the G-men had got them to "submit" to a Federal police examination. However, this policy met with an obstacle in the form of a Labor Department regulation . . . entitling persons arrested for deportation to send for their lawyers immediately. Some of the Labor Department subordinates disliked this regulation, and the GID [Hoover's division] itself protested strenuously against it after its experience in seeking confessions from the prisoners secured in its first raid . . . ; seven weeks later, just before the next raid, the regulation was revoked.

Though Hoover is still the same man he was in 1920, it is only fair to acknowledge that the Bureau's interrogation and other techniques have changed a great deal. And while the Bureau did not follow the *Miranda* code prior to *Miranda*, neither did any other police agency. Because its interrogation techniques have been superior to those of other police, it is worth examining them and examining how *Miranda* is likely to affect them.

In the usual case, FBI agents do not initially take a man

into custody for questioning but instead interview him at his home or place of work. They ask him casually about the offense, not probing too deeply on the first try. The agents do not bully or browbeat the suspect into incriminating himself. They operate on precisely the opposite theory, that the suspect's normal reaction will be to try to exculpate himself. Rarely will the suspect refuse to talk at all, for he fears that this will be taken by the agents as an admission of guilt.

Since the instinct of the guilty man is to throw the agents off the track, he will invent an alibi or otherwise falsify minor details of his knowledge of the victim or the circumstances of the crime. The precise content of the lie is unimportant. When the FBI agents return for a second interview, they will have established the lie and compiled a dossier, impressing the suspect with the scope of their knowledge. Catching the man in his first lie is the wedge which will ultimately produce the confession.

How can the agents wait for a second interview? What of the danger that the suspect will flee? Lack of anxiety in the detection of crime is a key to the Bureau's effectiveness. It requires a certain detachment to feel sure that a man under suspicion will not flee. But experience teaches that flight is not the natural tendency. Most of the crimes which the Bureau investigates, contrary to common belief, are petty crimes—for example, auto thefts and thefts from railroad cars. There is no pressure from the community for immediate solution of these crimes. Bank robberies and kidnappings represent only a tiny fraction of the Bureau's work. Even in serious crimes, most suspects do not flee when they are under suspicion, since this is a clear sign of guilt. Usually they assume, unwisely, that they can bluff it out. Behind the agents' coolness in trapping a suspect is also the knowledge that if he does skip, the Bureau has a superefficient network for tracking him down.

On the second meeting, the agents might suggest to the suspect that they believe he is lying and that if he wants to convince them otherwise, he might like to submit to a lie-detector test. Again, many will consent, afraid of the implication if they refuse. Once the test is administered, it is relatively simple to use it as the final wedge to extract the confession. Working in this way, the FBI can obtain confessions without the use of coercion, threats, or even trickery in the usual sense. And—here is the rub—if they do not get a confession, they may temporarily drop the case. The Bureau's superlative batting average is hardly an accident. It is a tribute not only to superior investigation techniques but also to a high degree of selectivity in charging crime. The suspect who is questioned without being booked cannot hurt the Bureau's batting average.

What effect will *Miranda* have on the Bureau's techniques? It is the essence of *Miranda* that the suspect not feel compelled to talk and that adverse inferences not flow from his failure to do so. Referring to the Bureau's pre-*Miranda* practices, Justice Harlan said: "[T]here is no indication that FBI agents must obtain an affirmative 'waiver' before they pursue their questioning. Nor is it clear that one invoking his right to silence may not be prevailed upon to change his mind." A truly effective self-incrimination warning might weaken the Bureau's opening device in questioning. Making clear to the suspect that he is entitled to a lawyer before he talks, even if he cannot afford one, could put an end to the interrogation. To avoid this result, it will be claimed that the initial interview at home or work constitutes "general questioning . . . in the fact-finding process," in the language of the opinion, and not a deprivation of the suspect's "freedom of action."

Thus the safeguards of the new code would not apply. Here is an area for litigation, with defense counsel expected to argue that confronting a suspect with an FBI badge is "inherently coercive" and the FBI arguing that the defendant was not a suspect at the time of the interview.

The second stage of the FBI's pre-*Miranda* practice—where the suspect "volunteers" to come to the Bureau—is likely to be restricted under *Miranda*. This may leave the FBI with false exculpatory statements (e.g., a false alibi) as the main confessional material. Such statements can be effectively used to prove guilt, so that the FBI conviction rate may not be seriously impaired by *Miranda*.

"A recurrent argument made in these cases," the Chief Justice wrote, "is that society's need for interrogation outweighs the privilege. This argument is not unfamiliar to this Court." He went on: "Although confessions may play an important role in some convictions, the cases before us present graphic examples of the overstatement of the 'need' for confessions." The Court then reviewed the other evidence: "Miranda, Vignera, and Westover were identified by eye witnesses. Marked bills from the bank robbery were found in Westover's car. Articles stolen from the victim as well as from several other robbery victims were found in Stewart's home at the outset of the investigation."

But the Court selected these four cases for appeal from some one hundred and forty confession cases. In possessing other, nonconfessional evidence, they are not necessarily typical. The Court would have been more candid if it acknowledged that the *Miranda* rule might mean the sacrifice of some convictions but that this was the price of protecting civil liberties. By not responding directly to

66

arguments of necessity, the majority tacitly accepts the dissenters' dark picture of the crime emergency. "The Court is taking a real risk with society's welfare," Justice Harlan warned. "The social costs of crime are too great to call the new rules anything but a hazardous experimentation." Aware that attempts statistically to prove a crime wave are also hazardous, Harlan in an oral statement relied instead on irrefutable "common knowledge."

Justice White accused the majority of returning the killer or rapist "to the streets and to the environment which produced him to repeat his crime whenever it pleases him." As a consequence, he predicted, "there will not be a gain but a loss in human dignity." For White, the Court had undermined "the most basic function of any government, [which] is to provide for the security of the individual and his property." This definition was not new. In his 1965 message launching the new war on crime, President Johnson put it in these words: No right "is more elemental than the right to personal security, and no right needs more urgent protection. . . . Our streets must be safe," the President said, "our homes and places of business must be secure." Only six months before, Barry Goldwater had called "security from domestic violence the most elementary and fundamental purpose of any government."

Of the four cases decided in *Miranda,* the one which most clearly reflects this concern for security is *Vignera* v. *New York*. It is also a case which evokes little sympathy for the accused. Vignera was a thirty-one-year-old laborer with a high-school education. On October 11, 1960, Vignera robbed the small Brooklyn dress shop of Harry Adelman. At knifepoint, he took from Adelman and others in the store some travelers' checks, a credit card, and other items. He was arrested a few days later when an associate tried to use the credit card; he was identified in a lineup by the victims, was interrogated, and confessed.

Vignera's case came up for trial before Judge Samuel S. Leibowitz, probably one of the century's best criminal lawyers and surely one of its most punitive trial judges. When it came to the confession question, Leibowitz charged the jury in language which belongs in the famous-last-words category:

> The law doesn't say that the confession is void or invalidated because the police officer didn't advise the defendant as to his rights. Did you hear what I said? I am telling you what the law of the State of New York is.

In the Supreme Court the *Vignera* case was argued for the people by William I. Siegel, a veteran appellate lawyer in the Brooklyn district attorney's office. Siegel is known in New York as a temperate and philosophical advocate—obviously rare qualities for a prosecutor. He approached the case with restraint, experienced in the foibles of humanity, which includes not only criminals and policemen, but judges as well. Siegel sincerely felt that the Court was moving too far in accommodating the rights of individuals to those of the community. But unlike other prosecutors before the Court, Siegel did not sound the war cry. He did not, even as the Court's dissenting colleagues did, threaten the justices with dire consequences if they voted to reverse. Indeed, he saw the handwriting on the wall and simply pleaded with the Court not to make the decision retroactive, a plea which the Court ultimately followed, to avoid "seriously disrupt[ing] the administration of our criminal laws."

"Does man live alone or is he a member of the community?" Siegel asked rhetorically. Justice Abe Fortas, who had listened patiently to the two days of often tedious argument, took up the question. He told Siegel he was troubled hearing lawyers who posed the issue as if it were merely a matter of convicting the guilty. Reaching for some meaning in the cases that went beyond police interrogation, Fortas asked Siegel whether in fact they were not dealing with "the relationship of the state and the individual," not just the criminal and society. Fortas spoke of the Magna Carta and other testaments to individual liberty. Siegel acknowledged that these were noble ideals but suggested that the immediate objective was to provide security, so that people have a chance to strive for these ideals. Fortas was not convinced, nor was the majority of the Court.

Certainly *Miranda* means something in terms of security. The difficulty is in defining whose security is paramount. To the majority, security means protection against the dangers of abuse of power. To the dissenters, it is the security of person and property from the threat of the predatory. Each man has his own set of insecurities. The probability that any of the dissenting justices would be victim of a violent crime is slim. To a middle-class shopkeeper in a poor urban neighborhood—such as Harry Adelman—the probability of becoming a victim is naturally greater. But the likelihood of personal attack is obviously not the index to a man's attitudes toward crime, which are largely irrational. The insecurity of libertarians, likewise, has its irrational side. Being a "cop-hater" has less to do with one's experience with police than with response to authority. Middle-class whites who make up the civil-liberties movement are usually not imprisoned falsely or subjected to the third degree. Their identification with the victims of police abuse may be as much a commentary on their own psyches as it is on the activities of the police. Are the police, then, simply scapegoats? No, but as the most visible symbols of authority they are the obvious target for hostility directed against authority.

The police alone are not responsible for the third degree, though abuse naturally would not occur without their willingness to participate. But who is guiltier of an atrocity, the interrogating policeman or the well-dressed prosecutor who arrives at the station house to take a suspect's statement after the interrogator has broken him down? Guilt can also be assigned to the community which closes its eyes to the means used by law enforcers. In the twenties some felt that popular hysteria over crime pushed the police into using the third degree. The Court in *Miranda* may be responding to a similar phenomenon, hoping to counteract mounting pressures on the police before brutal practices become institutionalized. The opinion is also a reminder that the nature of means differentiates democratic from totalitarian systems. All systems define their ends in high moral terms; the only test of character, then, is the methods chosen to reach these ends.

New York Police Commissioner Howard Leary has called *Miranda* a "sophisticated law for an immature society." But this criticism misses the point. That the Court is ahead of popular currents is hardly an accusation of misconduct. Indeed, it is when the Court ceases to lead and educate that the quality of our society is in danger.

4

Headlines
and
Headhunters

To fulfill his ambition for higher office [the prosecutor must] give the people what they want, and more; and there are no rungs in the ladder of fame upon which lawyers can plant their feet like the dead bodies of their victims.

—Clarence Darrow

When a New York prosecutor left his job to campaign for Congress, he released a statement of his qualifications. Topping the list was a credit for helping to convict Joe Valachi; toward the bottom, a reference to meritorious service in the Korean war. Placing the crime war ahead of a real war was not an accident.

Prosecutors are notoriously underpaid, yet no one has any trouble recruiting them. Why is this so? Because the job is worth so much in terms of publicity values. For the ambitious lawyer-politician, no other public office offers such a chance for headlines. In *An American Tragedy*, based on an actual murder case, Theodore Dreiser describes the elation of a small-town prosecutor when he smells the prospect of a sensational trial: "If he could only catch such a reptilian criminal, and that in the face of all the sentiment that such a brutal murder was likely to inspire! The August convention and nominations. The fall election." A little exaggerated, but not much. Witness the conduct of District Attorney Jim Garrison in the Clay Shaw prosecution.

Periodic efforts are made to curb abuses of publicity (Chapter 5), but the nature of the prosecutor's office continues to resist change. There are almost three thousand county prosecutors in the United States. Adding all the attorneys prosecuting cases in municipal and police courts, there are many times three thousand. Yet despite the number of prosecutors and their importance, little progress has been made in professionalizing the office, far less than in the case of the police. Police conduct affects many persons on a daily basis and has deep social impact, but the prosecutor too wields great power. The police may decide not to arrest—and thereby shut out prosecution—but once they do arrest, it is up to the prosecutor to seek criminal sanctions, which may mean destruction of a career or loss of liberty or even life.

There are many outstanding career men in police work, but few in prosecution. Recently the President of the National District Attorneys' Association asked: "How many young lawyers consider a career in the administration of criminal justice as a goal rather than merely a passing stage in their legal careers?" He added: "Prosecutors concentrate on performance in the courtroom, as they should, but virtually ignore the other aspects of criminal justice." It is no mystery why the prosecutor ignores everything but his courtroom role. It is in the courtroom where he gets the public eye and the headlines that promote his political career.

Though the great majority of criminal cases are bargained away or dismissed, a number still go to trial, usually a jury trial. Roughly eighty percent of all the criminal jury trials in the world take place in the United States; in New York City alone there are some three thousand criminal jury trials each year. The survival of the American jury system is tied to the political nature of criminal prosecution. The jury is an electorate before whom the prosecutor exercises his skill in manipulation, perfecting the style which will carry him to higher office. Every summation to a jury closely resembles a campaign speech in its appeal to emotion and prejudice. Patriotism continues to be the prosecutor's stock in trade. "I say to you with all the sincerity at my command," declaimed the Tennessee prosecutor in the Hoffa jury-fixing case, "that Chattanooga survived Chickamauga and Missionary Ridge. But Chattanooga could never survive the acquittal of those who have been proven guilty of contaminating the source of justice in our state."

"Trial by jury is melodramatic," Judge Jerome Frank has written. "Take the jury out of a trial, and most of the drama vanishes. Much of the tension disappears. The atmosphere becomes calm." American lawyers are impressed by the rational and undramatic quality of British justice. The fact that the jury has largely gone out of style in Britain has much to do with this quality.

When a prosecutor campaigns for reelection—as he must do in all but four states—or for election to higher office, he runs on his record, as well as on his past headlines. A high record of convictions is easily achieved by settling most cases—by making the disposition attractive enough so that the defendant takes a guilty plea in order to avoid jail, or at least avoid a long sentence. Quantitatively the results look good; qualitatively no one bothers to analyze them. This system leaves the prosecutor free to concentrate on "big" cases, like violent crimes which make headlines and agitate the public. What the Wickersham Commission found almost forty years ago remains largely true today:

> The "responsibility to the people" contemplated by the system of frequent elections does not so much require that the work of the prosecutor be carried out efficiently as that it be carried out conspicuously. Between the de-

75

sire for publicity and the fear of offending those who control local politics, the temptation is strong to fall into an ineffective perfunctory routine for everyday cases with spectacular treatment of sensational cases.

In contrast to most states, prosecutors in the federal system are not elected. United States attorneys, some one hundred throughout the country, are appointed by the President. The men chosen are usually outstanding lawyers who have backed the right candidate for the presidency. They tend to be older, more prestigious than state prosecutors. Yet they, too, are often concerned with political advancement, if not to elective office then to coveted judgeships. Because the office is controlled by the spoils system, there are few professional prosecutors. Turnover of U.S. attorneys with each administration is justified on the ground that the job is "politically sensitive," an admission of the partisan uses to which the prosecutor's office can be put.

Federal prosecutors rarely get involved in murder or rape cases, which make headlines for local district attorneys. But there is a counterpart in organized-crime and white-collar-crime prosecutions, cases in which the D.A. claims not simply to protect the community from dangerous persons but to preserve its moral health as well.

With crime-fighting a means to a political end, the prosecutor often has a great stake in conspicuous success; this, in turn, makes for anxiety in performance. The canons of ethics and the Supreme Court tell the prosecutor that his interest "is not that [he] shall win a case, but that justice shall be done," even if the defendant is acquitted. His political instinct—and the careers of predecessors—tell him otherwise. The real rewards are reserved for the prosecutor who gets convictions. The public has little interest in losers. Part of my own indoctrination as an assistant U.S. attorney was to attend weekly staff meetings where the boxscore of convictions was reported and the victorious prosecutors applauded. A novice soon gets the point that despite rhetoric about justice, what counts is the result.

If results count so much, then at least the real criminals are hunted down, or are they? In criminal prosecution, as in politics, it is the appearance of success that matters. The prosecutor must look good. The community has too little information to make intelligent judgments about the quality of results. Public ignorance tempts the prosecutor to exaggerate his victories. In 1936, for example, the public was told that the highest level of New York's underworld had been dealt a death blow by the conviction of "vice czar" Nicholas Montana. Montana was sent off to a stiff term in Sing-Sing after a long-winded denunciation by the district attorney. Only a few months later the illusion was shattered when Special Prosecutor Thomas E. Dewey convicted Lucky Luciano, for whom it turned out Montana had been a mere "messenger boy."

The prosecutor has an innate talent for manufacturing crises. Police are torn between the need to assure the public that matters are in hand and the temptation to use crisis to expand their powers. The prosecutor suffers no such split. He is not expected to maintain public order. He uses crisis as an invitation to keep hunting, not as a demand for responsible administration. And though he functions in the public arena when he tries a case, most of his work is completely invisible. Thus he has the enviable role of taking credit when the crooks are caught while avoiding censure when they are not.

The war against organized crime is a convenient vehicle for one seeking public acclaim. It is self-sustaining, a cold war in which the prosecutor can look good without having to achieve final success. The elusive nature of the enemy and his hidden conspiracy guarantee that the prosecutor can never win and at the same time that he will not be blamed for falling short of victory. The Mafia has helped to create many public heroes. In one case it almost created a President.

In the early 1950's Senator Estes Kefauver launched a legislative crusade on organized crime. It centered on the gambling syndicates, which allegedly financed underworld operations, and on the ties between the underworld and local politics. If the Kefauver hearings presented a threat to the Democratic city machines, it was not an accident. Only by disrupting the existing bases of power could Kefauver (a maverick) hope to capture the 1952 nomination.

Little of the information Kefauver dug up was new. One of his big exposés in New York, for example, was an incident showing Frank Costello's influence on judgeships. But the incident had been publicized almost ten years before Kefauver's hearings came to the city. The fact that its material was old did not stop the Kefauver investigation from getting top billing wherever it went. Allen Barth called it "the outstanding theatrical production of the 1950–51 season." Television was an indispensable ingredient. (Remember the movement of Costello's nervous hands as he repeatedly took the Fifth Amendment.) Kefauver pooh-poohed any claim that televising the hearings violated any constitutional rights of his witnesses. But witnesses who refused to testify because of television were vindicated. In quashing contempt citations, a federal judge wrote that the atmosphere of the hearings prevented a calm and truthful consideration of the facts, "the only reason for having a witness on the stand."

After the investigation ended, Kefauver published a

patently political book about his experiences. The introduction praised the Senator for resisting the "temptation to become a publicity grabber," but also said that "Kefauver's capture of the public imagination was spectacular." Noting that a lot of Kefauver-for-President clubs had spontaneously sprung up, the introduction concluded: "Though the Senator himself says he wants no part of it and is not seeking the presidency, anything can happen. Political lightning definitely has struck the man from Tennessee."

The text of Kefauver's book was expectedly homespun. He said that his committee "uncovered the ugly, dirty truth about the infection of politico-criminal corruption that is eating away at the strong, healthy tissues of our nation," and expressed concern over "the terrible power and ruthlessness of the enemy we are fighting. . . ." The approval of the people "has made me feel small and humble—but proud of the task I had been given to do." The book ends with a quote from a man in Georgia who wrote Kefauver: "John Doe on Main Street, U.S.A., Henry Roe on Broad Street, U.S.A., and all their cousins in Hickory Hollow have been shocked to learn of the conditions your Committee brought to light."

A decade later, in an unkind obituary for the Senator, *Time* magazine summed up the hearings:

> Gentle but relentless, Kefauver questioned them with painful sincerity, became to millions a pillar of log-cabin courage and small-town mores because of the contrast between his stolid ruggedness and the squirming, shifty-eyed hoodlums he confronted. From these hearings came no important legislation, few arrests, nothing very concrete. But his investigation did center national attention on big-time crime—and on Estes Kefauver.

79

One of Kefauver's "revelations" concerned an alleged Mafia meeting that had taken place in Cleveland in 1928. Joe Profaci, whose picture was taken at the meeting, was one of the witnesses questioned by Kefauver. Later the Senator revealed that Profaci "was unable to give a satisfactory explanation of his presence at the Cleveland convention"—almost twenty-five years before!

Six years after the Kefauver hearings, Profaci and more than fifty other persons were arrested in Apalachin, New York, at what was again alleged to be a meeting of Mafia overlords. For months afterward state and federal police, prosecutors, and grand juries conducted an inquisition to learn the purpose of the meeting. But they found out nothing. The most frequent excuse for being in Apalachin was to visit a sick friend, host Joseph Barbara. Profaci merely said he was visiting an "old friend." One witness claimed his car had broken down nearby, another that he had come for a good meal. (Barbara had ordered two hundred and forty-two pounds of meat to be picked up the day of the meeting.)

A year and a half after the meeting, twenty-seven men were indicted for federal conspiracy to obstruct justice and commit perjury. The charges related to the failure to disclose the real purpose of the meeting. The defendants were finally convicted after a lengthy trial in which the government's weightiest evidence was the two hundred and forty-two pounds of meat, indicating that the Apalachin meeting was planned in advance. The prosecution was one of the most elaborate in history, tying up some of the top trial lawyers in the country. The trial judge, Irving R. Kaufman, wrote articles and gave speeches complimenting himself on the way in which he had protected the defendants' rights. On appeal, however, all of the convictions were reversed.

The Court of Appeals found that there was no proof of a conspiracy—in other words, no proof that the defendants had agreed to lie about the purpose of the meeting. If the reversal seemed technical, it was pointed out that the purpose of the meeting may not have been to plan crime at all, but to desist from certain crimes. What troubled the court was not so much the lack of evidence at the trial but the fact that the prosecution had ever been initiated. Judge Charles E. Clark—former Dean of Yale Law School and hardly a friend of the Mafia—described the climate of hostility:

> From its inception this case was given unusual and disturbing publicity. . . . Much of this has been in terms of a crisis in law administration seemingly demonstrated by an unexplained gathering of arch criminals and of a general satisfaction that somehow they have met their just deserts of long imprisonment. This is vastly unfortunate; not only does it go beyond the judicial record necessary for its support, but it suggests that the administration of criminal law is in such dire straits that crash methods have become a necessity. But it seems we should have known better, and a prosecution framed on such a doubtful basis should never have been initiated or allowed to proceed so far.

Clark singled out for criticism two ex-prosecutors who published articles about the case while the convictions were on appeal. This criticism was unique. Usually only juries are shielded from prejudicial publicity, not appellate judges. What Clark's criticism meant was that judges are not deaf to public outcry and may be hesitant to spoil a victory by calling foul. Publicized praise of the Apalachin convictions created more pressure to uphold them, though the pressure was fortunately resisted by the court.

Mobs are not interested in justice, William O. Douglas has written. In the face of mob action, even the courts of last resort may hesitate to interfere. In Georgia's Leo Frank case the Supreme Court rejected defendant's claim that he was tried in an atmosphere charged with hostility, despite overwhelming evidence to support the claim. As Harry Golden describes the case in *A Little Girl Is Dead*, the people of Atlanta cheered when Frank was convicted of murdering a fourteen-year-old girl who worked in his factory. When Frank was sentenced to hang, there was wild celebration. In this instance it was not a prosecutor who made political capital of the case, but a newspaper publisher, Tom Watson. Watson staged a vicious campaign against "the perverted Jew," which succeeded not only in tripling the circulation of his newspaper but also in making himself a United States senator.

When the Frank case reached the Supreme Court, the Court refused to acknowledge the unfairness of the trial, piously reciting the case's procedural history as if observance of legal mechanics guaranteed fairness. "This is not a matter for polite presumptions," Justice Holmes retorted in dissent; "we must look facts in the face." He reminded the Court that the trial judge had suggested that Frank and his lawyer be absent when the verdict was returned, since there would be "probable danger of violence" if the jury did not convict. When the jury did convict, "there was such a roar of applause that the [jury] polling could not go on until order was restored. The noise outside was such that it was difficult for the judge to hear the answers of the jurors although he was only ten feet from them." Holmes continued: "[W]hen we find the judgment of the expert on the spot [the judge] . . . that if one juryman yielded to . . . reasonable doubt . . . neither prisoner nor counsel would be safe from the rage of the crowd, we think the presumption overwhelming that the jury responded to the passions of the mob." It is our duty to act upon this situation, Holmes insisted, "and to declare lynch law as little valid when practiced by a regularly drawn jury as when administered by one elected by a mob intent on death."

Holmes could little know how prophetic his words were. Several months later the Governor of Georgia, troubled by the unfairness of the trial and doubting the verdict, commuted Frank's death sentence. Instantly a mob formed, stormed the prison gates, and dragged Frank off and lynched him. So virulent were the passions that Tom Watson had whipped up, so outraged the popular sense of justice, that the Governor had to exile himself from the state in order to save his own life.

"[T]he deliberate use of a trial as a means of political education," writes an expert on the Soviet legal system, "threatens the integrity of the judicial process." Americans look with disdain and horror at the type of "show trials" which take place in the Soviet Union and other totalitarian countries. But the propaganda generated during our own trials of political enemies is almost on the same low level. In the first Smith Act trial against eleven Communist-party leaders, defense counsel tried to dramatize the bias-charged atmosphere by moving to hold the trial in Madison Square Garden. This facetious motion was naturally denied and the trial held in an ordinary courtroom. The manner in which it was conducted, however, had many features of the show trial.

The trial judge was Harold R. Medina. To be assigned the trial of a politically important case is high recognition and often a promise of better things to come. After the Communists were convicted, Medina was lionized by the public. The demand for his appearance at patriotic luncheons was insatiable, and he was tangibly rewarded by elevation to the United States Court of Appeals for the Second Circuit, the most prized judgeship in the country outside the Supreme Court.

But there was a rough spot on Medina's shining image. It was put there by Justice Felix Frankfurter. When the Supreme Court upheld Medina's contempt conviction of a Communist-party defense lawyer, Frankfurter delivered a biting dissent. The gist of it was that Medina had acted more like a partisan than a judge during the Communist trial. The record showed "numerous episodes involving the judge and defense counsel that are more suggestive of an undisciplined debating society than of the hush and solemnity of a court of justice." Medina's actions "weakened the restraints of respect that a judge should engender in lawyers"; he "thought defense counsel were in a conspiracy against him . . ."; and generally set a bad example in his conduct of the trial. It is true that Medina received threatening letters during the trial, and on one occasion his wife appeared in court and asked that a bodyguard be appointed to protect him. But defense counsel assured Medina that they and their clients had received many more threatening letters than he had.

An even more striking example of the merger of prosecutive and judicial roles is found in the Rosenberg espionage case. The case also illustrates that once the public is educated to take the hard line, its hostility cannot easily be turned off. When Judge Irving Kaufman sentenced Julius and Ethel Rosenberg, he set in motion a chain of events which inevitably led to the electric chair, though neither he nor the prosecution desired this result. What Judge Kaufman hoped to do by imposing the death sentence was to coerce the Rosenbergs into exposing the true dimensions of their spy plot. Such an exposé would have made Kaufman and the government prosecutors national heroes. But the strategy misfired; the government had not bargained on the fanaticism of the defendants.

Once the death penalty was imposed, however, a climate was created which made the sentence difficult to overturn. In a large sense Kaufman and the prosecution had played into the hands of the Communists, who, many felt, wanted the Rosenbergs to become martyrs. Massive rallies throughout the world, condemning Americans as murderers, only stiffened official will and narrowed the chance of compromise. Eisenhower inherited the Rosenberg case when he became President. He was inclined to commute the sentence on humanitarian grounds but was persuaded by his advisers (especially Attorney-General Brownell) that commutation would give the appearance of being "soft" on subversion. On the night of the execution large crowds gathered outside the White House, and when the official moment came there was cheering and honking of horns.

Judge Kaufman had told the Rosenbergs:

> I consider your crime worse than murder. Plain deliberate contemplated murder is dwarfed in magnitude by comparison with the crime you have committed. . . . I believe your conduct in putting into the hands of the Russians the A-bomb years before our best scientists predicted Russia would perfect the bomb has already caused, in my opinion, the Communist aggression in Korea, with the resultant casualties exceeding 50,000 and who knows but that millions more of innocent people

may pay the price of your treason. Indeed, by your betrayal you undoubtedly have altered the course of history to the disadvantage of our country. No one can say that we do not live in a constant state of tension. We have evidence of your treachery all around us every day—for the civilian defense activities throughout the nation are aimed at preparing us for an atom bomb attack.

Fifteen years later we know that Judge Kaufman's theory was preposterous, that the secrets allegedly passed had little scientific value; yet the Rosenberg case was not an aberration. Americans have always reacted in this way to exaggeration of the Communist threat. The Communists have stolen our most precious (and dangerous) secrets and will turn them against us. They are also poisoning the rest of the world against us. One can see the trend in a huge map—viewed by millions of visitors to the FBI in Washington—with the "Free World" diminishing in size and their world expanding. Color it red. Richard Nixon explained it to the House of Representatives after he exposed Alger Hiss: the increase in size of the Communist world was due to Hiss's presence at the Yalta Conference.

Public enemies are convenient; without them there would be few public heroes. The more important and threatening the enemy, the greater the victory. One prosecutor with a genius for inflating enemies and manufacturing crises was Roy Cohn. Just before he joined Joe McCarthy, Cohn worked on an investigation of subversion in the UN. In presenting his report to a federal judge, Cohn announced that it was "probably the most important investigation ever conducted in the entire history of the United States." But this was mild compared to his conduct a few years earlier as a twenty-one-year-old prosecutor.

In one of his first cases, Cohn delivered a courtroom harangue against a pathetic postal clerk who had admitted filching a small sum from the mails. In the speech (to which the local press had been invited) he painted the defendant as a dire threat to the entire American system. For those who saw the performance, Cohn's and McCarthy's later antics over Dr. Irving Peress, a "subversive" Army dentist, were no surprise.

The prosecutor "may prosecute with earnestness and vigor," the Supreme Court has said, "but while he may strike hard blows, he is not at liberty to strike foul ones." The rule is easier to state than it is to enforce. In the heat of contest, the foul line is easily crossed, particularly where the prospect of punishment is slight and the reward for victory great. During the Rosenberg trial, for example, U.S. Attorney Irving Saypol publicly announced that he had indicted an important member of the spy plot for refusing to testify in the Rosenberg case. This statement suggested (to jurors who learned of it) that the indicted man's testimony would have backed up the government's case against the Rosenbergs. After the conviction, the Court of Appeals called Saypol's statement "reprehensible," but this did little to hurt the former prosecutor, who by that time was safely ensconced in a judgeship, his reward for victory.

Not all prosecutors are of the headhunting or headline-hunting variety. A notable exception is New York's Frank Hogan. In a county known for its strong partisanship, Hogan continues to be reelected without opposition. He is so busy running his office that he has not tried a case for twenty years—proof that the big need in urban prosecution is effective administration and intelligent policy making, not sensationalism. Hogan's nonpartisan role in

New York is not a tribute to local political machines but to his own disinterest in higher office. Ten years ago Democratic senatorial nomination was thrust upon him. Though chief prosecutor of the most important district in the state—if not the nation—Hogan's name was unknown to most voters. His defeat in the election was the best evidence that he had never used his prosecuting office for personal publicity.

Many years ago, before bar associations got serious about regulating prejudicial publicity, Hogan adopted his own policy of declining to disclose the contents of defendants' statements in order to protect the right to a fair trial. For this he was condemned by many newspapers. Now efforts are being made to impose on all prosecutors the kind of restrictions which Hogan adopted voluntarily (see Chapter 5). Mandatory rules are necessary, because the prosecutor seeking favorable publicity cannot be expected to risk displeasing the press by adopting his own nondisclosure policy.

Passage and enforcement of such rules may have long-range benefits apart from protecting the defendant's right to a fair trial. If criminal prosecution ceases to offer easy opportunities to make headlines, then it will also cease to be a favorite route to higher office. Changes in the selection process might then produce and promote more dedicated career men of the Hogan stripe.

After a decade of reporting on the American legal scene, *The New York Times*'s Anthony Lewis went to England as a correspondent. He was at once impressed by the difference in the quality of criminal-law administration. "In Britain," he wrote, "politics scarcely intrudes into the courtroom. . . . There is no band of aggressive young prosecutors trying to climb the political ladder by making big cases. There are no judges trying to ascend the judicial ladder on spectacular criminal trials."

It would be oversimplifying the problem, however, to say that the divorce of crime and politics alone explains the superior quality of British justice, just as it would be unrealistic to assume that adoption of publicity restrictions will suddenly create a new breed of American prosecutors. The "answer to most of our problems," said Justice Holmes, "is for us to grow more civilized." When Holmes made this statement more than fifty years ago, he thought we were at least moving in the right direction. Now even that is uncertain.

5

Controlling Crime News

I cannot agree to uphold a conviction which affirmatively treats newspaper participation instigated by the prosecutor as part of "the traditional concept of the American way of the conduct of a trial." Such passion as the newspapers stirred in this case can be explained (apart from mere commercial exploitation of revolting crime) only as want of confidence in the orderly course of justice. To allow such use of the press by the prosecution . . . implies either that the ascertainment of guilt cannot be left to the established processes of law or impatience with those calmer aspects of the judicial process which may not satisfy the natural, primitive, popular revulsion against horrible crime but do vindicate the sober second thoughts of a community.

—Justice Felix Frankfurter

Four days after the assassination of President Kennedy, *The New York Times* published a letter from its own managing editor, Turner Catledge. Catledge wrote that a *Times* news report had erred when it referred to Lee Harvey Oswald as "President Kennedy's assassin." Said Catledge: "Although Oswald was accused of the assassination and the Dallas police thought they had an air-tight case against him, he was never tried and convicted. Under the American system of justice, he is innocent until proved guilty. Future articles and headlines will reflect that fact."

While such posthumous regard for Oswald's rights is overdone, it reflects growing concern with standards of crime reporting. There are more significant issues of public affairs, yet because the prerogatives of the press are involved, few issues have generated so much newspaper space and such heated debate. In response to the Warren Commission report, and with tensions heightened by a spate of sensational trials, the legal and journalistic professions have been groping for standards which will bridge the uneasy gap between the constitutional rights of the press and those of the accused. In 1966 an American Bar Association committee drafted a code to regulate

93

crime publicity which met with almost uniform condemnation by newspaper publishers and editors. Last summer the code was discussed at the ABA's annual meeting in Hawaii, and on February 19, 1968, it was adopted by a near unanimous vote of the House of Delegates, the ABA's legislative body. The vote came despite frantic lobbying of news media representatives. Whether the code will be followed by State bars remains to be seen.

The publicizing of sensational crime is as old as crime itself. In America, with its dual institutions of trial by jury and assertive journalism, the key issue is the influence of publicity on the minds of jurors. One critic posed it this way: "In the case of a particularly audacious crime that has been widely discussed, it is utterly impossible that any man of common intelligence, and not wholly secluded from society, should be found who had not formed an opinion." This was in 1846. During the newspaper circulation wars at the turn of the century, Arthur Train called yellow journalism the "most vicious factor in the administration of criminal justice." Train damned the newspapers for creating false sympathy for defendants rather than bias against them. This does not change the issue; it simply illustrates a difference in environment.

Each decade has had its *causes célèbres*, and each *cause célèbre* has produced a wave of revulsion and talk of curbing excessive publicity. But it has remained just that—talk—with no tangible reforms. This time has been different. The ABA committee, known as the Reardon Committee, after its chairman, Massachusetts Justice Paul Reardon, spent two years studying the problem. It found that most prejudicial material is not the result of independent news reporting but originates with law-enforcement officers and lawyers (especially prosecutors). Hence the committee recommended strong controls over all participants in a criminal case. Its theory is that by drying up the source, most offensive material will not find its way into the newspapers.

A strongly-worded canon of ethics will bar lawyers' statements about the following: a defendant's prior criminal record or information as to his character or reputation; the existence or contents of any confession; the performance of any examination or tests or the defendant's refusal to submit to such an examination; the testimony of prospective witnesses; the possibility that the defendant will plead guilty; and any opinion as to the defendant's guilt or innocence, although a defense attorney may state that his client denies the charges. During the trial itself, no lawyer can release or authorize any statement relating to the case, except that he may quote from or refer without comment to public records in the case. Lawyers who violated the canon would be subject to disciplinary action, which could mean suspension or disbarment.

The Reardon Committee assumes that since most offensive publicity comes from the mouths of the trial participants, controlling them will indirectly cure abuses by the press. But what happens when the press acts on its own, when an editor personally initiates a prosecution? This was pretty much the situation in the *Sheppard* case. Federal District Judge Weinman, in reversing Dr. Sheppard's conviction in 1964, sized it up accurately in these words:

> If ever there was a trial by newspaper, this is a perfect example. And the most insidious violator was the Cleveland *Press.* For some reason that paper took upon itself the role of accuser, judge, and jury. The journalistic value of its front page editorials, the screaming, slanted headlines and the nonobjective reporting was nil, but

> they were calculated to inflame and prejudice the public.
> Such a complete disregard for propriety results in a
> grave injustice not only to the individual involved but to
> the community in general. . . . If ever a newspaper did
> a disservice to its profession; if ever the cause of freedom
> of the press was set back, this was it.

But if the identity of the villain was clear to Judge
Weinman, it was not to the Supreme Court. Its forty-page
opinion in the *Sheppard* case does not so much as mention
the Cleveland *Press* or its editor, Louis Seltzer, the man
responsible for the Sheppard vendetta. Instead, the villain
in the eyes of the Court is the trial judge, Edward Blythin
(since deceased). It was Blythin's "failure to insulate the
proceedings from prejudicial publicity and disruptive influence [of newsmen in the courtroom] which deprived
Sheppard of the chance to receive a fair hearing." How
Blythin, who did not enter the case until months after the
Press had done its damage, could have insulated the proceedings is a problem in metaphysics which the Court does
not resolve.

The *Sheppard* opinion found it unnecessary to consider
"what sanctions might be available against a recalcitrant
press." In its anxiety to evade this issue, the Court
scrambled for a precedent, some authoritative guide that
would get it off the hook. The most authoritative thing
available was the Chief Justice's own Warren Commission
report. Not bothered by dissimilarity in the cases, the
Court proceeded to build the flimsy *Sheppard* structure on
the Warren foundation. It is obvious from reading the
opinion that Justice Clark, its author, not only had the
Warren report at his elbow as he wrote; he also literally
tore some pages from the report and called them the
Sheppard case: "[N]either the press nor the public had

the right to be contemporaneously informed by the police or prosecuting authorities of the details of the evidence being accumulated against Oswald [Sheppard]." And again: "Bedlam reigned at the courthouse [read "police station"] during the trial and newsmen took over practically the entire courtroom, hounding most of the participants, especially Sheppard." Clark does not tell us that the entire courtroom consisted of four rows, so it was impossible for newsmen not to take it over.

Bending over backward to avoid offending the press, the Court virtually sat on the trial judge. Rarely has appellate hindsight mustered such a catalog of "should-have-dones." The judge should have considered locking up the jury during the trial, though Sheppard's counsel advisedly refrained from requesting it. He should have granted the defense motion to change the place of trial, though as one justice indicated during the oral argument, no county in Ohio was free from the poisonous publicity. The judge should have postponed the trial until after local elections, in which he was running to succeed himself. But the election actually took place during jury selection and before the trial began, so the purpose of a short postponement is unclear. Finally, the Court condemned the trial judge for "requesting" rather than "warning" the jury not to read newspapers during the trial.

Without specifically referring to the *Sheppard* opinion, the Reardon Committee doubted the efficacy of these remedies. "None of these techniques," it said, "can at the same time (1) assure a fair trial in the face of prejudicial disclosures that saturate the jurisdiction and (2) preserve other rights of the defendant and the right of the people to see that the guilty are properly punished." The Committee illustrated its point with the following examples:

A continuance, if it is to be long enough to dissipate the effects of the potentially prejudicial publicity, may require the defendant to sacrifice his right to a speedy trial. And its purpose will be defeated if the publicity is renewed when the case finally comes up. A change of venue may also require the sacrifice of state or federal constitutional rights [as will waiver of jury trial] and will undoubtedly be ineffective if the case is one of wide notoriety. Voir dire [examination of prospective jurors] . . . cannot fully cope with a juror's failure to be candid or with influences that occur below the level of consciousness. Sequestration [locking up the jury during the trial] does not remedy the effects of pretrial publicity and may itself prejudice the defendant because of the inconvenience and annoyance to the jurors. Admonitions to the jury have often proved ineffective [as conceded by almost half the judges responding to the Committee's poll].

If the Supreme Court thought the restricted scope of the *Sheppard* opinion would be understood or its professional courtesy to the press reciprocated, it was due for disappointment. The President of the American Society of Newspaper Editors said the opinion would "hide from public knowledge virtually all of the facts of law enforcement and the administration of justice." He called it a step in the direction of the English rule, where the contempt power is invoked freely against journalists. Misunderstanding of the *Sheppard* case reached crisis proportions when a Harvard law professor, Arthur Sutherland, told a conference of state trial judges that the opinion invited them to use the contempt power against the press. Although justices are not accustomed to interpreting their opinions publicly, the professor's statement was too much for Justice Clark. Addressing the same conference the next day, Clark protested. It's all a mistake, the Justice declared. The Court didn't say anything about the contempt power, or set standards for the press. Perish the thought. The Justice even denied that the Court intended to prescribe rules for judges: "We laid guidelines the court *might* follow, not guidelines they *must* follow."

Even this unusual effort at clarification did not dispel the misunderstanding. Some judges continued to read the *Sheppard* opinion literally. At Sheppard's own retrial, for instance, the new judge (having read what Clark said about "bedlam") refused to give seats in the courtroom to any but local newsmen or wire-service representatives. Reporters from such national publications as *Life* and *The New York Times* had to wait in line daily beginning at seven-thirty A.M. in order to compete with curious housewives for the few vacancies in the courtroom. Those who left their seats to meet a deadline did so at the risk of losing them. Some days these reporters did not get in at all.

Only a month after the *Sheppard* case was decided by the Supreme Court, an event occurred which was to throw an already fuzzy subject into a state of confusion. On July 14, 1966, eight Chicago student nurses were slain in their dormitory. Effective police investigation quickly produced a suspect, Richard F. Speck, whose fingerprints were found in the dormitory and who was identified from a photograph by the lone survivor. Speck's photo was plastered on every front page as a massive manhunt began. As a result of this publicity, he was soon recognized by a physician treating him after a suicide attempt.

In April, 1967, Speck was convicted of the eight murders and sentenced to death. Since prejudicial publicity is likely to be an argument on appeal, it is worth examining what that publicity was. First, were news disclosures before Speck's arrest proper? The Reardon report would permit the police to release any information necessary to aid in apprehending a suspect or warning of any dangers he may present. Clearly there is a public interest in stopping a dangerous criminal before he commits further violence. Thus the Chicago police acted properly in publishing Speck's picture and conducting the manhunt. It was not necessary, however, to announce positively and repeatedly that Speck was "the killer" nor to disclose all the damaging evidence against him, especially the fingerprint evidence (the accuracy of which became a key issue at the trial). Even if disclosures were necessary to aid in Speck's apprehension, public interest in the disclosures ended when he was arrested. Here, however, Police Superintendent Orlando Wilson compounded earlier injury by adding even stronger public assurances of Speck's guilt. (Later Wilson was invited to address the Publishers Association convention, where he commiserated with newsmen as fellow victims of the Supreme Court and its decisions "designed to suppress the truth.")

As the trial date approached, the judge—Herbert C. Paschen—granted a change of venue from Chicago to Peoria, though any difference in the degree of news coverage in the two cities was doubtful. Shortly before trial, Judge Paschen issued a fourteen-point order regulating reporters. It covered everything from sketching in the courtroom (prohibited) to the consequence of visiting the men's room during trial (loss of one's place). The most serious point ordered reporters to print only what occurred in open court (a ban going far beyond anything recommended by Reardon). To make this worse, reporters were forbidden to purchase trial transcripts—a strange way to ensure the accuracy of their reports. These restrictions were all the more arbitrary in view of the jurors' sequestration, meaning they could not have access to newspaper reports. As the trial approached, and the judge was subject to unanimous condemnation and lawsuits from the press, he retreated one by one from many of his fourteen points. It was still necessary, however, for the state's highest court to rule, in a suit by the *Chicago Tribune*, that reporters could buy official transcripts anytime they wanted to.

The *Speck* case represents a good argument for the adoption of the ABA code regulating publicity before and during trial. Without clear guidelines, the tendency of any trial judge, particularly in this era of close appellate oversight, is to err on the side of caution. Had the Reardon proposals been in effect in the Illinois courts during the Speck trial, the fourteen-point fiasco would never have occurred. All of which suggests that definite standards may be the press's best protection against arbitrary obstruction of newsgathering.

It took six weeks to pick a jury in the *Speck* case, longer than it took to try the case. Partly this was because of the enormity of the crime; one murder gives each side twenty peremptory challenges; eight murders required one hundred and sixty. A "peremptory" challenge is exercised without stating any reason. It differs from a challenge "for cause," which the court exercises; there were also many of these in the *Speck* case, on grounds of opposition to capital punishment or an acknowledged belief in Speck's guilt.

For a crime like the Chicago massacre, this six-week ritual is perhaps inevitable; the Reardon rules would not avoid it. Indeed, by setting higher standards for jury selection, they might actually lengthen the *voir dire* process. A prospective juror who has formed an opinion about the defendant's guilt will be dismissed "unless the

examination shows unequivocally that he can be impartial."
And any juror who remembers any significant prejudicial
information will be excused despite his testimony that he
can be impartial. The *voir dire* examination in the *Speck*
case might still be going on, were these rulings in effect,
which only emphasizes the need to concentrate on the
early stages of a case, before publicity has done its damage.

The whole emphasis in Reardon is on indirect controls
over publicity. Only in the rare, perhaps nonexistent case
is there an attempt to restrict the press directly. This is
for flagrant abuses which actually affect the jury's verdict.
And the regulation is even more narrow than it seems, for
it will apply only to articles written when a jury trial is
already in progress. Even the kind of pretrial poisoning
which took place in the *Sheppard* case, which many journalists concede was contemptuous, will be immune from
punishment.

Despite its modest nature, the Reardon report outraged
the journalistic community. The President of the American
Society of Newspaper Editors, for example, called it
"selection of news, suppression of news, censorship of
news," leading to "abuse and confusion," "misguided,
quixotic, unnecessary and harmful to our democratic
system." *The New York Times's* A. H. Raskin has criticized
his colleagues' reaction to the report, their "tendency to
take refuge in self-serving sloganeering." Most of the
Reardon proposals were opposed by the American Society
of Newspaper Editors and the American Newspaper
Publishers Association. One tactic of these groups was
to deny the existence of a problem, claiming a failure to
show any real damage from crime publicity. Actually the
Reardon Committee based its recommendations on a
study of hundreds of reported decisions, on extensive inter-

views with trial participants, and on its own content analysis of crime-news coverage in more than twenty cities during a one-year period (1965). While the Committee concedes that the *percentage* of cases with a serious publicity question is small, it shows that the *number* of such cases is substantial, far greater than has been generally believed.

Some critics of the Reardon proposals, such as the *Washington Post*'s Alfred Friendly, saw dangers "in the excuse they may give to the police for suppressing what should not be suppressed and what the Reardon group is perfectly willing to have released." The impact of the regulations on southern civil rights cases was the specter most often raised in opposition. Railroading of Negro suspects and cover-up of white murderers are what the report was charged with abetting. The truth is that the report is largely irrelevant in these cases. If the Reardon regulations are not available, the red-neck sheriff will find some other excuse for secrecy, or he will simply dismiss reporters without any reason.

On the other hand, sanction against flagrant press abuses may never be imposed in the South, since contempt punishment must come from the local judiciary. A good—or bad—example is the newspaper in Lynchburg, Virginia, which during the trial of a Negro defendant repeatedly printed that his northern lawyer was "linked with Communist-front organizations." These articles may be bad enough to get the defendant's conviction reversed, but the reversal will not deter the newspaper, as the threat of contempt might.

That the news media's use of civil-rights cases in opposing Reardon was propagandistic is shown by their capacity to quickly shift ground. In August, 1967, when press spokesmen tried to persuade ABA members to abandon the Reardon report, they argued that the proposed rules would stifle news about the criminal records and conspiratorial activities of urban rioters.

In February, 1967, another in the series of press-bar reports came out. This one was by a committee of the Bar Association of the City of New York, chaired by seventy-eight-year-old Judge Harold R. Medina of the federal Court of Appeals. The Medina report differs from the Reardon report primarily in denying power to hold news media in contempt. Judge Medina concluded his report "with a feeling of optimism," which proved to be misplaced. The judge was sure that the reluctance shown by news media was due to a threat to their independence and constitutional rights. "Once it becomes firmly established that these fundamental rights are not in jeopardy and that their contribution to the purification of the judicial process is a voluntary one . . . their cooperation will be more generously forthcoming." Like Justice Tom Clark before him, Medina was unprepared for the press's ungenerous treatment. "A code of silence," a "policy of secrecy in law enforcement," said the American Society of Newspaper Editors. "Frankly, I think those people don't realize who their friends are," Medina lamented.

The Editors' group believes that "putting prior restraint on news sources is equivalent to putting prior restraint on the press." What the drying up of "live" sources really means, however, is that the laborious task of digging out the facts must be done independently. Independent reporting of crime news is now largely a myth, according to a leading trial lawyer, Milton R. Wessel. He writes, "A large number of criminal indictments themselves would go completely unnoticed if not highlighted by a tip from the police or the district attorney, and sometimes by the defense counsel." Getting crime news without assistance between indictment and trial is even more difficult. "Absent an official tip of some kind, the reporter has no way of knowing what applications or motions will be heard." And covering the trial, says Wessel, is the most difficult, time-consuming job of all. "The press can't afford to assign full-time reporters . . . to any but the most exceptional cases. Stenographic transcripts are much too expensive, usually not available in time, frequently incomprehensible without exhibits and long study."

Recognizing that without help, publicity will be limited, participants in a trial often point out to the press significant matters in the record, advise them when an "interesting" witness will testify. These officials, says Wessel, adopt "the fiction that they are merely reciting what is public, ignoring that it is not otherwise available and in any event they are editorializing by selecting episodes that they consider favorable. These comments . . . actually serve to create partisan news and prejudicial comment, which for practical reasons would never otherwise exist."

This is not just theory. Wessel's point was proven in a long criminal trial in which both he and this author participated. At Wessel's request, the trial judge directed all participants to withhold any comment concerning the case until its conclusion. No restriction was placed upon the press itself, but it was arranged that "off-the-record" tips, summaries, and digests would not be given to reporters, nor would anyone furnish free copies of transcripts to them. Despite the newsworthiness of the case, writes Wessel, "the amazing result was that there was absolutely no public comment anywhere about it for over a month following the beginning of trial." When one reporter finally did come upon the case, it was so difficult for him to follow that he ended up writing his articles on the theme "No Publicity in Fraud Trial." Wessel does not suggest that drying up present sources will foreclose press coverage; he believes, on the contrary, that it will encourage the press to select and concentrate on those cases which are truly newsworthy.

Despite scary predictions that we are moving toward the British system of strict press controls, there is little in the ABA's new code that is remotely suggestive of the British system. For one thing, besides marked differences in social and political conditions, the legal conditions for the contempt power in England make sanctions possible that would never be dreamt of here. There is no constitutional guarantee of free press, and reporters and editors may be punished without having threatened any "clear and present danger" to justice. In fact, they may be punished simply for outraging the dignity of the court, regardless of any prejudice to litigants.

The British themselves have been showing signs of discontent with the way in which press controls have been operating. Insulation of criminal trials from prejudicial publicity—in notorious cases like that of Stephen Ward or Dr. John Bodkin Adams—has been more theoretical than real. The press may report anything which takes place at a preliminary hearing, a pretrial inquest to decide if there is enough evidence to hold a defendant for trial. Much of this testimony may be inadmissible at the trial, but the press is free to report it anyway. In the case of Dr. Adams, who was ultimately tried for poisoning an elderly patient, charges of similar murders had been aired at the preliminary hearing and widely publicized before trial. Last year a bill was passed by Parliament which practically did away with the preliminary hearing, in part because of its abuse for publicity purposes.

The American press says it is fighting for "the public's right to know." To know what? That Sam Sheppard slept with his lab technician, or that young Dr. Coppolino had an affair with Mrs. Farber? The very pettiness of most crime news, the poverty of examples of important exposures, both suggest that the press-bar fight has been inflated.

If the new ABA code threatens anything, it is loss of circulation. Even this is not a necessary result. Newspapers which rely on sensational crime stories to keep up readership will simply have to work harder to find out the facts of these stories. Overlong dependence on official handouts may have made reporters lazy, but it gives them no constitutional right to maintain the handouts.

If the press is determined to carry out its "watchdog" function, nothing in the new regulations stands in its way. There are many dark areas of politics and crime in need of biting investigation—most of them outside the police station and the courtroom. It is hardly the modest self-restrictions adopted by lawyers that are muzzling the press. The real sources of news suppression are more subtle. Andrew Kopkind has described them:

> In ways which journalists themselves perceive only dimly or not at all, they are bought, or compromised, or manipulated into confirming the official lies: not the little ones, which they delight in exposing, but the big ones, which they do not normally think of as lies at all, and which they cannot distinguish from the truth.

Now that lawyers are finally showing some initiative in putting their own house in order, the press might do well to follow the example.

6

Another Look at the Enemy Within

If the Government becomes a lawbreaker, it breeds contempt for law; it invites every man to become a law unto himself; it invites anarchy. To declare that in the administration of the criminal law the end justifies the means—to declare that the Government may commit crimes in order to secure the conviction of a private criminal—would bring terrible retribution.

—Justice Louis D. Brandeis

The FBI's Assistant Director, Cartha deLoach, recently attacked America's "malignant disease" of defiance to law. DeLoach, who considers himself J. Edgar Hoover's heir apparent, pointed to a common denominator between real criminals and peace and civil-rights demonstrators. All these people believe they are above the law, he said. If in fact they do have this belief, they are in powerful company. For the FBI and many other police agencies also consider themselves above the law.

Ex-FBI agent William Turner has described a letter of commendation he once received from J. Edgar Hoover. The letter thanked Turner for his work "in an operation of considerable value to the Bureau in the security field." Hoover praised "the competent, resourceful and effective fashion in which you handled your responsibilities, [which] contributed materially to the successful handling of this delicate assignment." The delicate assignment, Turner tells us, was to break into a private home and plant an electronic bug.

In 1966–67 the government had to confess error in a

score of cases because of the FBI's illegal eavesdropping. These electronic-eavesdropping activities have been well publicized. Actually, however, they are conducted on a small scale compared to the activities of human eavesdroppers—informers. The use of informers by the FBI and other police agencies raises as many troubling questions of law, ethics, and morality as the use of electronic devices. All large law-enforcement agencies have their slush funds to buy information, and much of it comes from criminal informants who are allowed to engage in crime under protection of the police. Some idea of the widespread nature of the practice is indicated by an FBI report crediting seventy-five hundred arrests in a recent year to information furnished by the Bureau's "criminal informants." The practice is not new. Sixty years ago Stanley Finch, the first Chief of the Bureau, boasted to Congress that some of his best leads in enforcing the Mann Act came from madams who spied on their rivals and turned the information over to the Bureau.

The term "informer" is used generically to embrace a whole cast of related characters. The late Professor Richard Donnelly described them as follows:

An *informant* is one who, having participated in an offense, turns against his partners and discloses information to the police. Quite often, under a promise of immunity, he testifies against them at their trial. The *police spy* enters into conspiratorial plans for the purpose of obtaining information. His connection with the police antedates his participation. His role is primarily that of an observer and reporter. The *stool pigeon* acts as a decoy to draw others into a trap. He solicits the commission of a crime. His part is that of a catalyst. The *agent provocateur* is a specialized and sophisticated stool pigeon traditionally employed by the political police. He joins an organization such as a labor union or political group in order to destroy it. By pretended sympathy with its aims he leads its members to commit crimes so that they may be apprehended and punished.

An informer must be distinguished from an undercover agent, a policeman who disguises himself as a criminal in order to infiltrate behind enemy lines. He may become important in the criminal machinery, but he remains a government employee, working only one side of the street. The informer, on the other hand, lives in a tenuous world of shifting allegiances, depending on who rewards or intimidates him.

Undercover agents themselves are not immune from taint, particularly those who work in streets among prostitutes, gamblers, and dope peddlers. That vice-squad officers often succumb to vice themselves is one of the best-known but least publicized facts about law enforcement. But sometimes there is an unconscious suggestion. A recent Sunday supplement piece glamorizing undercover agents states:

> The Narcotics Bureau fights most of its campaigns from the inside, behind the enemy lines. . . . N-men are picked not only for their razor-sharp wits and ice-cold nerve but also for their ability to mix in the underworld without suspicion. . . . As undercover men, narcotics agents learn to look like gangsters, talk like gangsters, think like gangsters. . . .

Even if vice-squad officers resist corruption in the form of bribery, they do not resist it in the methods of trapping their prey. In prostitution cases, writes Judge John M. Murtagh, New York's former chief magistrate, many vice officers "act on their moral certainty of a woman's guilt

[and] do not hesitate to invent evidence on which she would have to be convicted. . . . They would probably go on to say that the question of whether a prostitute is guilty of a specific offense on a specific occasion is basically academic. But—is it? Can we trust our police always to protect the innocent if they do not respect the rights of the guilty?"

In a vice case, often the only possible defense is "entrapment." Entrapment is the conception and planning of an offense by a police officer and its commission by a person who would not have done so except for the officer's trickery, persuasion, or fraud. The classic entrapment case, *Sorrells,* arose out of prohibition. An undercover agent prevailed upon the defendant's sympathies to obtain some liquor for him. Supreme Court Justice Roberts described the circumstances in an angry opinion:

> [D]efendant had no previous disposition to commit [the act] but was an industrious, law-abiding citizen, [whom] the agent lured . . . to its commission by repeated and persistent solicitation in which he succeeded by taking advantage of the sentiments aroused by reminiscences of their experiences as companions in arms in the World War. Such a gross abuse of authority given for the purpose of detecting and punishing crime, and not for the making of criminals, deserves the severest condemnation. . . .

Widespread disgust with this type of corrupt practice of prohibition agents was one of the main factors leading to repeal of the prohibition amendment.

In Philadelphia several years ago the police selected a group of attractive young women as undercover narcotics agents. The method of operation was to accost a man and suggest that he could obtain her favors in return for getting her some narcotics. It is easy to see how this approach could lead an otherwise innocent man into committing a crime. But most narcotics defendants are addicts themselves and cannot succeed with the defense of entrapment. They are ready and willing to accept the offer to commit the crime. For this reason smalltime addict-sellers are sitting ducks for narcotics agents. As Judge J. Skelly Wright of the U.S. Court of Appeals has said:

> [N]arcotics arrests, as distinguished from other offenses, are shaped by the police, at the time of their choice, against a suspect of their choice, before witnesses of their choice. Thus, the Government has almost total control of the . . . situation.

Undercover narcotics agents work constantly with informers. Perhaps no other police work uses so many informers, so many in fact that it is not unusual for a state agent to arrest a man who happens to be working as federal informer and vice-versa, or even for a federal agent to arrest a man working for one of his colleagues. The argument in favor of narcotics counterespionage is that informers are needed to catch the big suppliers. In the mythology of law enforcement this is one of the more outrageous myths. Big suppliers operate remote from the street, behind a series of protective screens next to impossible to penetrate. It is the little men, as Judge Wright suggests, who are easiest to catch.

It is particularly easy to recruit informers in narcotics cases. Harsh mandatory penalties are normally fixed for narcotics convictions—e.g., five years with no chance for parole under federal law. But the prosecutor has discretion to charge the offender with some lesser crime or not to charge him at all. Under these conditions, almost any-one caught selling dope can be terrorized into "cooperat-ing." Usually the informer is charged with a crime just to assure his continued cooperation. His release comes only after he has performed to the authorities' satisfaction.

Most informers do not end up testifying in court. Their normal function is to give the police leads to other evidence. The government keeps its informers under wraps for several reasons. In the first place, exposing the in-former means subjecting him to possible harm, including death. There is less concern for the individual than for the system of detection in which he is deemed indispensable. Police who depend on a network of informers cannot afford a reputation for a high rate of informer mortality.

A more covert reason for keeping informers out of court is that jurors might not convict if they got a close look at the state's methods. Jurors usually presume that a defendant is guilty—contrary to the theoretical presump-tion of innocence. But a feeling that the state's witnesses are liars or otherwise shabby characters may shake that presumption, cast doubt on the prosecutor's honesty, and generally taint the state's case. This is what happened in the Candy Mossler trial, in which defense counsel con-vinced the jury that state witnesses were trading their testimony for shorter prison terms.

The practice of sparing one criminal to catch another is an old one. Two centuries ago in England a convict got an automatic pardon if he informed on his accomplices. Under special laws in some jurisdictions the prosecutor can formally grant immunity from prosecution to a witness who testifies against others. But informal grants of immu-nity are more common. In the Hoffa case, for instance, government informer Ed Partin, had an indictment for misuse of union funds over his head. Since Partin helped convict Hoffa, the indictment has not been tried, and it is a safe guess that it never will be.

Using a friend to trap a friend is not an unusual practice for police and prosecutors. Pressure will even be exerted on a witness to betray a member of his own family. A bizarre example was David Greenglass, whose testimony in the Rosenberg spy trial was responsible for sending his sister to the electric chair. In the Smith Act cases it was revealed that several FBI informants who had infiltrated the Communist party actually recruited relatives and friends to join the party and then turned their names over to the Bureau.

FBI informants who join the party do not always turn out to be reliable. A man named Mazzei was employed for twelve years in this capacity. His big moment came in 1953, when his testimony convicted a group of third-string Communist leaders for teaching violent overthrow of the government. After that he capitalized on his experiences and was a favorite witness at congressional hearings. But a few years later when the Communist case reached the Supreme Court, the Solicitor General shattered the FBI by admitting that Mazzei was a perjurer. One of the things that convinced the Solicitor was Mazzei's 1956 testimony that the party planned to assassinate a number of government officials, to blow up bridges, and to poison reservoirs. The Court threw out the Communists' convictions, commenting wryly that Mazzei had "poisoned the water in this reservoir."

In dealing with an informer, stool pigeon, or other "cooperating" witness, the prosecutor develops a proprietary interest in him. As they fight the common cause, the witness is part of the team, and his past crimes are seen in a different light. There are mitigating circumstances and explanations. The prosecutor's subjective approach is typified by the Assistant U.S. Attorney who described the informer-witness in a tax prosecution as an "honest, honorable American citizen" doing his patriotic duty in testifying for the government. A year later when the same witness appeared for a defendant, he was "a black marketeer and a perjurer and almost anything you can name."

Sometimes a cooperating witness so dominates the scene that he may look as if he's running the prosecution. In the United Dye stock-fraud case—the longest federal trial on record—the government's chief witness, Alexander Guterma, was on the stand for three months. It is not hard to understand how a prosecutor comes to regard as indispensable a man on whom so much depends. The fact that Guterma was the genius behind the fraud, testifying against less-culpable men, did not prevent their conviction. In the adversary system the prosecutor's goal is to make a case against the man on trial, not to present an objective picture of what happened.

Few prosecutors actually suborn perjury by deliberately asking a witness to tell a false story. They can often obtain the result they want without having to go this far. The resourceful criminal who becomes a cooperative witness knows that he is expected to get his former associates convicted. That knowledge is enough to shape his testimony, aided by suggestive questioning by the prosecutor.

An informer's cooperation is rewarded by the prosecutor. *The New York Times*'s Sidney E. Zion quotes an anonymous "prosecutor from a large Eastern city," who says: "I take good care of my informants. I pick a judge who I know cooperates with our office and I can tell the informer exactly what he's going to get." The prosecutor also boasted of being able to arrange for the informer to go to a prison of his choice. "I even worked it for one prisoner to stay where he was. It wasn't much of a place, but they wanted to move him and he didn't want to go because he was near his mother who used to bring him candy all the time."

The government will also go to great lengths to protect its witnesses. For instance, in a recent federal case in New York the defense hired a private investigator to watch the comings and goings of the government's main witness, on whom the case rested. The prosecutor unsuccessfully protested to the judge, accusing the defense attorney of obstructing justice (a federal crime). This objection was ironic because in a previous case the same prosecutor had a defendant tailed for an entire year, taking motion pictures of him whenever he emerged from his house. A curious double standard.

The long war between Robert Kennedy and Jimmy Hoffa illustrates this double standard. The first round was the 1957 trial of Hoffa for bribing an investigator for the McClellan Committee. Kennedy was the chief counsel for the Committee. Hoffa allegedly tried to "plant" attorney John Cye Cheasty on the Committee as a counterespionage agent. Cheasty told Kennedy about it and he arranged to hire Cheasty and permit him to take Committee documents. The FBI was alerted, and immediately after Cheasty passed the documents to Hoffa, Hoffa was placed under arrest. For a private citizen to put a paid informer on the government's payroll is a crime. But five years later when Kennedy's men did the same thing in reverse, they committed no crime, at least not according to the Supreme Court.

The informer within Hoffa's camp (during his 1962 Nashville trial for a Taft-Hartley violation) was Edwin Grady Partin, boss of a Baton Rouge local and close associate of Hoffa for some five years. Partin stayed with Hoffa during most of the Nashville trial, was one of his trusted inner circle, while all the time he was reporting daily on Hoffa's activities to Kennedy's men. Most of his reports involved attempts to bribe jurors. That was in the fall of 1962. A year and a half later Partin made his appearance in court as a witness for the government in the jury-fixing trial. Hoffa was dumbfounded. An endless series of hearings, charges, and countercharges followed, the main thrust being that Partin should not be allowed to testify because of the way in which he got access to Hoffa. The trial judge admitted Partin's testimony, and Hoffa was convicted. In December, 1966, the Supreme Court upheld Hoffa's conviction, finding no violation of his constitutional rights in the government's use of Partin.

The 1957 bribery charge was interesting because it influenced the pattern of Kennedy's later campaign to put Hoffa in prison. Hoffa was acquitted of the charge and two months later went on to win the presidency of the Teamsters. Kennedy felt that the government had poorly prepared the case. Another lesson was derived from Hoffa's trial on wiretapping charges in 1958, in which he was acquitted. During the trial a juror was excused after disclosure that he had been "approached." There was no proof that the approach had come from Hoffa, but the incident alerted Kennedy to another area to watch.

When Kennedy became Attorney General he set up an elite team inside the Justice Department to work on Jimmy Hoffa and his men. The team was headed by Walter Sheridan, an ex-FBI man, and consisted of about a dozen lawyers, as well as investigators and other personnel. Sheridan answered directly to Kennedy, although there was a criminal division within the Department and a section in charge of organized crime. Within Justice, Sheridan's men were known as the "Hoffa group," though the existence of the group was seldom acknowledged outside the Department. During its lifetime the group chalked up more than one hundred Teamster convictions. But so far as Sheridan and the group's top legal talent were concerned, getting Hoffa was their full-time job.

"Sheridan knew from the beginning," wrote *Life* after the conviction, "that anything less than a total, prolonged effort, a war of attrition—a 'vendetta,' according to Hoffa— would have resulted in more acquittals, more hung juries." There was no room for doubt of Hoffa's evil "in the good-guys-and-bad-guys-only world that Walt Sheridan inhabits with Bob Kennedy."

Into this world one day in October, 1962, walked Edward Grady Partin, the man who was to hand Hoffa on a silver platter to Kennedy and Sheridan. When Partin first made his appearance in the Kennedy camp, it might have been hard to tell him from one of the bad guys. He had a long criminal record and for years had been one of Hoffa's roughest henchmen. By the time Partin had finished his work as Kennedy's informer two years later, he was a hero.

The picture of Partin which emerges from the thirteen-page *Life* article is that of a bad boy who somehow got religion. The photographs show him as a devoted father, a handsome ex-prizefighter, a responsible union executive. The most appealing thing about Partin's story was the motive that finally turned him against Hoffa. He says he was revolted by Hoffa's suggestion that he throw a bomb at Bobby Kennedy's house, which would endanger the lives of the Kennedy children. Partin got no money for the *Life* article. "I want this story to put enough backbone in other Teamsters so they'll stand up and kick Hoffa out of our union."

Against this picture of Partin, the "good guy," there were certain other facts which magazine publicity could not hide, though it attempted to color them. Partin did

121

Hoffa's dirty work "without any hesitation." This meant using "any tool you can get, from a sawed off shotgun to some crooked cop or politician." Hoffa trusted him with "ticklish jobs" and always paid him well for them. There was a familiar note to Partin's explanation. In the Hoffa world "you're either one thing or another, and I was a Hoffa man."

Most of the thousands of words of Partin's *Life* story was taken up with explanations for the dozen crimes which he has been charged with and in some cases convicted of. The intricacies of frame-ups, mistaken identities, and misunderstandings read like a bad soap opera. Even giving credit to these explanations, Partin's history as a hoodlum and bully is unmistakable. No amount of retouching could change this history. Nor could it hide the irony that Kennedy's high-purposed crusade to save the labor movement had come to rest on a man like Partin.

Partin was described in different terms in a Teamster magazine article published after the conviction. His sordid record was listed to show how unworthy of belief he was. Teamster members were apparently partisan enough to slide over the flaw in the article. For it was precisely because of his capacity for lies and violence that Partin had been so useful to Hoffa.

For his part, how did Partin rationalize his intimacy with Hoffa? He recognized that Hoffa was crooked, but "as long as I thought it would help the union," said Partin, "I'd do darn near anything he asked me to." This included bribing a Labor Board agent to fix union elections and using strong-arm methods to take over a rebellious local.

Finally revelation comes to Partin: "But the funny thing was that the better I got to know him, the closer we got; and the more he seemed to trust me and the more things I did for him, the more doubtful I got, I began to see Hoffa wasn't working for the Teamsters; he was working for Hoffa and for Hoffa's power."

Partin admitted that by the time he contacted Kennedy he had his "own good reasons for quitting Hoffa." He was knifed once, and shot at another time. He wondered whether Hoffa could have been behind these attacks. Another reason must have been the federal indictment for misuse of union funds, returned several months before. Partin knew the reputation of Sheridan's group, its box score of Teamster convictions, and must have realized that this was one rap he could not beat. In any event, the assassination story gave Partin a shrewd basis for approaching Kennedy, and he made the most of it. Like John Cye Cheasty five years before, he was moved by patriotism.

During the Nashville trial Ed Partin spent most of his time with Hoffa and his team of codefendants and lawyers. He always seemed to be around when Hoffa needed something done. During the trial Partin was in touch with Sheridan nearly every day. Sheridan told him not to report on Hoffa's trial strategy but only on jury tampering. Even then the prosecution was worried that the informer's interference with Hoffa's right to consult counsel might jeopardize a conviction.

In Partin's undercover work, security precautions were strictly observed. Partin and Sheridan met surreptitiously —almost always in an automobile. Sheridan's group had code names for the key characters. Partin was known as "Andy Anderson" and Jimmy Hoffa was labeled, not very deceptively, "Himself."

When Partin appeared as a surprise witness in the bribery trial, defense counsel tried to suppress his testimony. In the course of extended hearings that followed,

Sheridan was asked whether Partin was paid or promised anything for acting as an informer. Sheridan flatly denied that he was. Later a memorandum was discovered from Sheridan to the administrative chief of the Department of Justice requesting a payment of three hundred dollars per month. The payment was to be made to a Department attorney for delivery to an undisclosed person —later admitted to be Partin's estranged wife. Faced with the disclosure, the government claimed that this monthly sum was not "payment" to Partin but simply reimbursement for his expenses. Yet the three hundred dollars a month coincided with the amount of support payment Partin was obligated to make to his wife. Sheridan's direction that the money should come out of the Department's "confidential fund" was reminiscent of the 1957 bribery trial, when Hoffa testified that informer Cheasty was paid three thousand dollars out of the Teamster's "revolving fund."

Despite widespread opinion among lawyers that the Supreme Court would buy at least one of Hoffa's many arguments, the Court upheld the conviction. Only Chief Justice Warren and Justice Douglas were disturbed by the methods used to convict Hoffa, and only Warren voted to reverse. Douglas felt the Court should not rule on the case, since lower courts had found that Partin was not "planted" in Hoffa's camp by the government but went there voluntarily. The majority rejected this hair-splitting distinction, admitting that the government and Partin had connived from the first to inform on Hoffa. But the majority nevertheless went on to hold that Hoffa was simply the victim of "misplaced confidence" in Partin. This was the same as saying that none of Hoffa's rights had been violated.

The Chief Justice wrote an unusual opinion, basing his dissent solely on abhorrence that a conviction could be based on the testimony of a man of Partin's character. Acknowledging that credibility of an informer is a matter usually left to juries, Warren explained why the Hoffa case was different:

> Here the Government reaches into the jailhouse to employ a man who was himself facing indictments far more serious (and later including one for perjury) than the one confronting the man against whom he offered to inform. It employed him not for the purpose of testifying to something that had already happened, but rather for the purpose of infiltration to see if crimes would in the future be committed. The Government in its zeal even assisted him in gaining a position from which he could be a witness to the confidential relationship of attorney and client engaged in the preparation of a criminal defense. And, for the dubious evidence thus obtained, the Government paid an enormous price. Certainly if a criminal defendant insinuated his informer into the prosecution's camp in this manner he would be guilty of obstructing justice. I cannot agree that what happened in this case is in keeping with the standards of justice of our federal system and I must, therefore, dissent.

At the same time it affirmed Hoffa's conviction, the Court upheld two other convictions dealing with police espionage. In one case an undercover narcotics agent got access by false pretenses to the defendant's apartment, where he made a buy. In another, a Justice Department informer bugged conversations between himself and a Hoffa lawyer who was trying to bribe a juror. (Like Hoffa and Partin, the lawyer thought the informer was his employee.)

The Court's strong boost for the legality of informers may be a means of compensating for restrictions on the police in interrogation cases. Since the Hoffa opinion the Court has gone even further in sanctioning the use of informers, upholding a prosecutor's pretrial refusal to disclose the identity of his informer. Justice Douglas dissented sharply: "There is no way to determine the reliability of old reliable, the informer, unless he is produced at the trial and cross-examined. Unless he is produced, the Fourth Amendment is entrusted to the tender mercies of the police."

The Court's increased permissiveness toward informers coincides with another restrictive tendency—toward electronic eavesdropping. In the spring of 1967 in the *Berger* case it declared the long-standing New York wiretap statute unconstitutional, as amounting to illegal search and seizure. And a month later Hoffa's second conviction (for defrauding a Teamster pension fund) was sent back to the lower court to determine whether it was tainted by government eavesdropping on a codefendant. It is not easy to follow why evidence of a human eavesdropper should be legal and an electronic one not. The distinction seems to depend on the fact that one dealing with an informer "voluntarily" risks exposure, while the victim of electronic devices is unaware that his conversation is being overheard by third persons. Still, in ethical terms, at least, betrayal by a trusted friend seems more offensive than betrayal by an inanimate object.

Though restrictions on electronic eavesdropping have brought angry protest, the police actually have not come off badly in the bargain. Electronic devices are used in only a limited class of cases; the Court's approval of informers, on the other hand, affects wider levels of law enforcement.

What impact the informer cases will have on our society is another matter. They lend judicial cover to the already shadowy operations of the vice squads and the political police. The price of such secrecy is loss of scrutiny and public control over methods of enforcement. It tempts the police to suppress or manufacture evidence or to act on the basis of irresponsible accusations. The expanding definition of "security" expands the varieties of misconduct which can be hidden behind that label. The enemy within is not simply Jimmy Hoffa, or even Ed Partin, the informer. It is the tendency of men in power to abuse the excuse of "public necessity," to resort to criminal methods in the name of warring on crime. Said the late Justice Frankfurter:

> To approve legally what we disapprove morally, on the ground of practical convenience, is to yield to a short-sighted view of practicality. It derives from a preoccupation with what is episodic and a disregard of long-run consequences. The method by which the state chiefly exerts an influence upon the conduct of its citizens . . . is "the moral qualities which it exhibits in its own conduct. . . ." [Criminal prosecution] should not be deemed a dirty game in which the "dirty business" of criminals is outwitted by "the dirty business" of law officers. The contrast between morality professed by society and immorality practiced on its behalf makes for contempt of law. Respect for law cannot be turned off and on as though it were a hot-water faucet.

7

Justice
for the
People's Court

In the [lower criminal courts] there are more hurts to
the innocent and more trampling over basic individual
civil liberties and ethical considerations than you will
find in most police departments. Much of the concern,
energy, and effort that the courts expend with respect to
police conduct could better be spent getting their own
house in order. . . .

—Professor Fred Inbau

L ess than one mile from the majestic halls of the United States Supreme Court, with its landmark rulings for defendants' rights, lies the real world of criminal justice. Here thousands of persons—mostly Washington's poor—move, or are pushed, through the mill of mass-production justice. The place is called the Court of General Sessions; in other cities, the Municipal Court. The difference in name does not matter, for the quality of justice in these People's Courts is strikingly the same—miserable.

To the eighty thousand defendants ground through the mill each year (sixty times the number in the dignified District Court) high-court liberal decisions are meaningless. They have failed to touch the lower-court "system," where prosecutors have no time to prepare their cases (and may convict the wrong man), defense lawyers may not know their clients' names, and judges may send them to jail without knowing much more than their names.

The President's Crime Commission reported its shock at conditions in the lower criminal courts:

[The Commission] has seen cramped and noisy court-rooms, undignified and perfunctory procedures, and badly trained personnel. It has seen dedicated people who are frustrated by huge caseloads, by the lack of opportunity to examine cases carefully, and by the impossibility of devising constructive solutions to the problems of offenders. It has seen assembly line justice.

A central problem of many lower courts is the gross disparity between the number of cases and the personnel and facilities available to deal with them. . . . An inevitable consequence of volume that large is the almost total preoccupation in such a court with the movement of cases. The calendar is long, speed often is substituted for care, and casually arranged out-of-court compromise too often is substituted for adjudication. Inadequate attention tends to be given to the individual defendant, whether in protecting his rights, sifting the facts at trial, deciding the social risk he presents, or determining how to deal with him after conviction. The frequent result is futility and failure.

Washington's lower criminal court is no worse than any other city's. In some ways it is better. But what in other places may be merely a local disgrace, in Washington is a national disgrace. For Washington is a federal city, run by the President and Congress. The prosecutor in the Court of General Sessions is the mighty Department of Justice, whose offices are not far from the court, but whose efforts—and pocketbook—have been committed elsewhere. For years the chief of General Sessions (whose entire office had one secretary and a few old typewriters) begged the Justice Department for a more experienced staff and better working conditions. But nothing was done. The prosecutors were victims of the same neglect as the people they prosecuted.

Recently Washington has been taking a hard look at General Sessions. In 1966 the Department of Justice issued a report on the court by attorney Harry Subin, which was popularized by a crusading *Washington Post* reporter, Leonard Downie. The Subin report amounts to an indictment. A sample: "[P]roceedings in court are largely unintelligible to the layman. The court and all of the agencies which deal with it operate at such a frantic pace that the entire operation is dehumanized." Instead of blaming the system which inspires disrespect, says former Attorney General Katzenbach, we blame the poor, who are really victims of the system. But Katzenbach cannot get off the hook so easily. If the Crime Commission he chaired was shocked by the lower courts, it is because law-enforcement leaders like himself never made it their business to look inside these courts.

Washington is the country's largest city with a Negro majority. When one speaks of the poor in Washington, he is almost always talking about Negro poor. The Negro community long ago lost faith in the criminal justice system, if it ever had any. A Harris poll has shown that more than half of Washington's Negroes believe that local courts are prejudiced and inequitable. Concluded the pollsters: "[I]f it is true that whites tend to view the District crimes as Negro crime, then it is equally true that Negroes tend to view the law as the white man's law." The fact that until recently the law was administered almost entirely by whites did not help this image.

Not all of the Negroes meet the law as defendants; the majority who come to General Sessions are witnesses and complainants—victims or alleged victims of crime. The dehumanization which the Subin report deplored is nowhere more apparent than in the treatment of citizen complaints. Subin has described the "Counter," where thousands of such complaints were received as "a cross between the crowd at the race track teller's window on a warm summer afternoon and the accident ward of a metropolitan hospital." In a huge room prosecutors were separated from complainants by a long partition—the "Counter." There police officers and store detectives waited to present their cases, jammed in with dozens of private complainants, some still bloodied from a fracas, and shouting defense lawyers, together with relatives of those involved, who were busy caring for infants or scolding small children. In the noise, which was often deafening, prosecutors were supposed to weed out the few cases which had merit from the many which did not. Privacy was impossible. "The most intimate details of family life, and of criminal charges, were aired in this atmosphere." Here is how Subin describes the range of complaints:

> [A] woman complains of a beating by her husband; a common-law wife wants her husband kept away from the house; a neighbor complains that the people next door are throwing trash in the alley, or making too much noise, or beating their children; a wife wants a divorce, or support payments; a senile man complains of being followed, and another wants the President arrested; a store owner wants a bill paid; a customer wants his repossessed goods back. And so it goes, day after day, year after year. People with legitimate complaints of serious crime; people who want to use the threat of prosecution to bolster their side of a private dispute; people with hallucinations; people with ugly, complicated, but essentially noncriminal domestic problems; and people who simply do not know where to turn. . . .

Most of the problems filtering through this and other lower criminal courts are not really criminal at all. They are social problems, and the court is being forced into the unwanted and inappropriate role of a social agency. Prosecutors hearing these complaints are neither social workers nor therapists; for the most part they are inexperienced young men just out of law school. They are not inclined—still less, qualified—to become mediators in the slum Negro's struggle with his family and with his environment. As a result, concludes Subin, "many confused, frightened, and troubled people are sent away without help."

When prosecutors (and judges) do make judgments about the people who come before them, particularly defendants, the judgments may be distorted by bias. As the President's Crime Commission stated:

> A prosecutor or judge with a middle-class background and attitude, confronted with a poor, uneducated defendant, may often have no way of judging how the defendant fits into his own society or culture. He can easily mistake a certain manner of dress or of speech, alien or repugnant to him, but ordinary enough in the defendant's world, as an index of moral worthlessness. He can mistake ignorance or fear of the law as indifference to it. He can mistake the defendant's resentment against the social evils he lives with as evidence of criminality.

The root problems of the lower courts are twofold. One is to find alternatives to criminal treatment for social problems. The second is to identify and reach defendants whose conduct actually represents a threat. President Johnson has stated that "the first offender's initial contact with our correctional system is often a turning point in his life." In the same vein, his Crime Commission found that "hardened habitual criminals do not suddenly and unaccountably materialize. Most of them committed and were brought to book for, small offenses before they began to commit big ones." If the lower criminal courts are not actually creating criminals, they are at least creating lives of crime. Nearly everyone agrees that these courts must be reformed, but the size of the job should not be minimized. Not only practices but personnel have become hardened, and both resist change.

The public thinks of a defendant in a criminal case as surrounded by safeguards (a belief which often leads to attack on "bleeding-heart" judges, "overtender" to the accused). If the picture of a system in which the accused has broad constitutional protection is true to any extent, it is a picture confined to felony cases. The "screens" which theoretically protect a felony defendant—grand jury, preliminary hearing, formal trial with a competent lawyer—are not available in the lower courts. Though the importance of these courts is greater—because of the immense numbers of persons affected—traditional rights are largely lost in the shuffle. Subin describes the typical process in General Sessions: It begins in the office of an Assistant United States Attorney. He decides what charges will be lodged against the defendant, a decision which "is made in a matter of minutes, in a hurried atmosphere, by a prosecutor who frequently has had very little experience." Though the prosecutor may not have all the facts, he has no time to fill in the gaps. In his haste he may overlook serious cases and prosecute trivial ones. "There is time in most cases only for reaction, not for reflection."

Once the charging decision is made, there will be no more investigation. Careless preparation may help the defendant; often it hurts him. If the case goes to trial, it is handled by a second prosecutor, who is not even familiar with the initial facts. He tries the case "out of the file," which is handed to him a few minutes before trial. In other words, he improvises. Often the defense attorney does not have the good sense, or interest enough, to ask the right questions, and the judge may be indifferent. Only after conviction may the prosecutor begin to feel uneasy about the flimsiness of the evidence or the credibility of an identifying witness.

To illustrate how informal a General Sessions trial can be: Once a prosecutor left the courtroom for a short time to interview some witnesses in the corridor. When he returned he found that his entire case had been put in evidence by the judge and that the defendant had already taken the stand and been examined. The prosecutor was just in time to cross-examine the defendant and hear the judge (who had actually prosecuted the case) pronounce him guilty. The same disorder can prevail at sentencing. One judge got so carried away in criticizing the victim of a stabbing (a husband who "hung around the house too much") that he forgot all about the defendant-wife and ended up sentencing the victim to prison. Less amusing is the General Sessions judge who occasionally sentences a convicted misdemeanant "to the electric chair," just to observe the defendant's horrified reaction.

Many of the court's serious misdemeanor cases start out as felonies. If they remained felonies, they would have to be sent to the "big court," the District Court, where maximum penalties run to many years. But few cases do stay as felonies. Sometimes the prosecutor uses the higher charge as a club to put the defendant and his attorney in a bargaining frame of mind. This is often a bluff, because the prosecutor knows he cannot get away with sending a lot of cases to District Court. The District judges will only bounce them back to General Sessions. They do not want the dignified image of the District Court tarnished with what they call "cheap" felonies. And they want to keep their caseload small. While the General Sessions calendar has been expanding enormously in recent years, the caseload in the District Court has remained remarkably constant.

Most of the serious misdemeanors involve thefts or assaults. About two thousand assault cases each year start out as felonies—assault with a dangerous weapon—but only some two hundred end up that way. The line between felony and misdemeanor is thin, even arbitrary. Often the divider is the number of stitches required by the victim. The current rule of thumb is fifty stitches for a felony, but it may vary from prosecutor to prosecutor. Even more arbitrary is the determination of who is the victim and who the assailant. Generally the first man taken to the hospital ends up as the victim; the latecomer gets charged with the assault. Casual judgments like this are not made in all assault cases, however. Mostly they are confined to intraracial Negro crime. Where the victim is a white man, the prosecutor's attitude is likely to be different.

Whether a felony charge will be knocked down to a misdemeanor by the prosecutor, or one of two misdemeanor counts dismissed, usually depends on the bargain arrived at between defense counsel and the prosecutor. Though the whole bargaining process usually lasts less than an hour—sometimes only minutes—this is often the only chance to learn what evidence the prosecutor has, and if the defendant is clearly guilty, whether any facts mitigate his offense. Such an inquiry may not be very thorough, but it may be exhaustive compared to a typical trial by a speed-demon judge.

What looks like a good deal to a defendant, however, may really be worth little. If a case was intentionally overcharged for bargaining purposes, reducing the charge is no real gain. Similarly, eliminating one of two charges may be an illusory benefit where judges do not impose consecutive sentences. Everyone involved in the process knows the score—except the defendant. He thinks he is getting something in return for his guilty plea and is willing to pay his lawyer a fee which has not been earned.

A few General Sessions judges actively promote guilty pleas. One openly threatens harsh penalties if a defendant goes to trial and is convicted. He prides himself on "keeping the calendar moving." Sometimes the court itself plays a role in the gamesmanship of plea bargaining. It does a variation of the Mutt-and-Jeff routine, in which a team of police interrogators, consisting of a "good guy" and a "bad guy," works upon the emotions of a suspect in order to induce a confession (see Chapter 3). What the court does is to assign a tough judge to sit in the trial part—an obvious threat of stiff punishment to those convicted—while keeping a lenient judge in the branch that takes guilty pleas. This technique invariably succeeds in cutting down the number of trials.

Most of the cases are defended by a small group of lawyers who make their living in the lower criminal courts. They are known as "regulars," or sometimes as "Fifth Streeters," referring to the courthouse street where many have their offices (though some seem to have offices only in their "hats"). Every large city has a band of marginal criminal lawyers who live off the poor because the system has not found a better way to defend them.

As the regulars sit on the "mourners' bench" at the front of court, they are assigned by the judge to defendants who appear without counsel. The defendants are not told that they will have to pay for legal services, but they soon find this out. The "conference" between the lawyer and his prospective client takes place in the makeshift cells behind the courtroom. The President's Crime Commission reports that it "has seen, in the 'bullpens' where lower court defendants often await trial, defense attorneys demanding from a potential client the loose change in his pockets or the watch on his wrist as a condition of representing him. Attorneys of this kind operate on a mass production basis, relying on pleas of guilty to dispose of their caseload. They tend to be unprepared and to make little effort to protect their clients' interests." If the amount of money the lawyer will take is surprisingly little, it is almost always matched by the quality of his representation. A defendant confined to jail while his case is pending may never see his assigned counsel. Recently one wrote to Chief Justice Warren to see if Warren could find out for him who his lawyer was.

Even when they are paid, few General Sessions attorneys investigate the facts of a case. And certainly not the law. When a new judge refused to appoint certain of the regulars, he explained his reason: "If I interrupted the proceedings to bring up an important question they overlooked, it was almost as if I had awakened them from a deep sleep." Recently one of the regulars was sentenced to jail for fifteen days for defending a case while drunk. Conscious of inferior defense representation, an occasional prosecutor will keep a weak felony case in General Sessions rather than let it go over to the District Court, where its flaws might be exposed by competent defense counsel.

To make the regulars scapegoats for the ills of General Sessions would be unfair, however, and a serious error. They are there because no one else wanted to be. Washington has more lawyers per capita than any other city in the world. Across town from grubby General Sessions, ensconced in plush office buildings, is Washington's version of Wall Street. The "uptown" lawyers mostly represent large corporations doing business with (or "getting the business" from) the government. They may take an occasional indigent case in the comfortable and familiar environment of the District Court (more often they send their young associates), but, as one judge remarked, "they wouldn't be caught dead in General Sessions!"

In a recent speech to the American Bar Association, former Attorney General Katzenbach asked why more lawyers did not involve themselves in the administration of criminal law. "No such conditions of neglect and widespread ignorance prevail" in commercial fields, Katzenbach remarked naïvely. He thought the fact that criminal courts handle *people*, rather than products, should make them all the more interesting to lawyers. Maybe. But the clients involved are usually not to the lawyers' taste. Besides, lawyers don't get rich on human interest.

Not that criminal law is entirely ignored by elite lawyers. But the problems that get their attention—and occasional *amicus curiae* briefs—are the grand issues of constitutional law. In the famous *Gideon* case, which established the right to counsel in every felony trial, the American Civil Liberties Union and other friends of the court were aided in the appeal by an army of top lawyers and had to turn some volunteers away (though the appeal was granted on a handwritten petition drafted by Gideon himself, with no legal help).

The *Gideon* case went to the heart of the adversary system. When a case is fought in a full-blown trial, there is no substitute for a skilled defense lawyer. But this kind of trial seems to be a luxury that our lower criminal courts cannot afford (and usually do not need). The constitutional lawyer with his elaborate briefs, and the master of trial strategy, is not at home in the lower courts. As an indication, until recently the District of Columbia Legal Aid Agency, the darling of Washington's legal establishment and one of the country's top defense outfits, stayed as far away as possible from the General Sessions Court.

And when one of the General Sessions judges appointed the President of the District Bar Association to defend a case, the defendant refused to accept his services. Much to the delight of the regulars, the defendant asked that one of them be assigned to his case.

For defense lawyers who know how to "negotiate the system," a major weapon is delay. Not delay for the purpose of investigation or developing defenses, but delay simply for the purpose of wearing down the prosecution. If witnesses have to keep coming back to court (losing their daily wages) while lawyers continue to get postponements, sooner or later they will stop coming. And the prosecutor will have to drop the case or allow the defendant to plead to some less serious offense. Sometimes a desperate prosecutor will call "ready" for trial, knowing his witnesses are absent, hoping the defense will not realize their absence and will "fold" (plead guilty). Often delay benefits only the lawyer. He may try to delay plea or sentence solely for the purpose of collecting his fee. A client is more amenable to payment when he is "under the gavel" than after he has been sent to jail. Judges often go along with the lawyer, even though they know the real purpose of adjournment. In General Sessions there is even a name for it—one hears an attorney brazenly ask for "an adjournment under Rule One."

The final test of lower-court justice is what happens to the defendant after conviction. On this test there is almost total failure. "A system which stresses speedy and summary disposition of cases," writes Subin, "cannot show much concern with the defendant himself." To some of the judges, the defendant is a statistic, not a person. Guilty pleas are allowed without knowing whether the defendant really understands the charge against him. An innocent man will rarely plead guilty, but many men do plead guilty to an offense more serious than the one they committed.

Some two thousand of the three thousand serious misdemeanants convicted each year in General Sessions go to jail. The court and the public are rid of them, but not for long. The local jail is a way station with no program for rehabilitation, no facilities, and no vocational training, except the criminal know-how that can be learned from fellow inmates. Most of the convicted men will return to court later on new charges; for some, serious ones.

General Sessions judges often sentence blind, with no more than a police "rap sheet" (a criminal record, often inaccurate) to describe the man before them. In the "big" court, which deals with felonies, ninety-five percent of defendants sentenced are investigated first by a professional probation staff. Serious offenders rate serious consideration from judges; minor offenders do not. It is too expensive. "A system that treats defendants who are charged with minor offenses with less dignity and consideration than those who are charged with serious crimes," says the Crime Commission, "is hard to justify." We know the cliché about an ounce of prevention, but we do not act upon it.

The probation staff at General Sessions until recently was skeletal and below standard. Each officer had about sixty probationers to supervise, more than twice the prescribed caseload. Ten years ago a District crime commission recommended that the staff be tripled, but the recommendation was not implemented. Even so, the Court of General Sessions is better off than the lower courts in most other jurisdictions, which have no probation services at all.

Many reforms of the lower courts have been proposed, but these measures will mean little without men of dedication and ability to carry them out. It is the trial judge who is the key to justice for the People's Court. The late Judge Jerome Frank coined the term "upper-court myth" to describe the misconception about the relative importance of appellate and trial courts. It is only in the lower courts that the judge and the public come in contact, and the experience largely shapes public attitudes about law and justice.

A case can be made, writes Professor Harry Jones in *The Courts, the Public, and the Law Explosion,* that a judge's importance varies inversely with his rank. A man unworthy by character and temperament to be an appellate judge, says Jones, is even more unworthy to be entrusted with the responsibilities of a trial judge. "He may be at the bottom of the judicial totem pole, but it is there that the exposure is often greatest and the strains of the judge's role manifest for all to see. . . . Nowhere in the whole range of public office are weaknesses of character, intellect, or psychic constitution revealed more mercilessly than in the discharge of the responsibilities of a trial judge." It is obviously important, Jones concludes, that the new judges brought to the lower criminal courts "not be professional misfits or clubhouse hacks." Yet distinguished lawyers have been discouraged from seeking judgeships by the Dickensian character of these courts, leaving the field open to mediocrities, and so perpetuating the poor quality of the courts.

Lately there have been signs that this chain of mediocrity is being broken, at least in Washington's Court of General Sessions. Last year when the chief judgeship of the court became vacant, President Johnson appointed Harold A. Greene to fill the job. Greene has been a General Sessions judge since 1965. In his first year in office, Greene awed the Washington community with the way he attacked his job. Coming from the Justice Department, where he headed civil-rights appeals and research and helped write the 1964 and 1965 Civil Rights Acts, Greene was accustomed to long hours, tough legal problems, and the facts of social injustice. In fact, his sense of injustice was developed early, as a Jew living in Nazi Germany.

In his first year Greene wrote hundreds of pages of legal opinions, in a court which had almost forgotten that judges could write. The subjects ranged from attack on the vagrancy laws (for punishing a defendant's status) to ordering payment of government funds for assigned counsel (promising more competent advice to indigents). But Greene made his deepest impression in the courtroom, where he treated each case individually, refusing to be pressured into snap decisions, even if it meant deliberating after the regular court hours. Other judges, used to the court's loose traditions, might have resented Greene's example, but resentment is difficult in the case of Greene, a soft-spoken man who avoids personal acclaim.

Since Greene has become chief judge, the probation office has been expanded, a new chief appointed, and professional standards developed. The office is now aided by an OEO-funded Offender Rehabilitation Project, headed by a highly qualified social worker and staffed partly by ex-offenders. With Greene's encouragement, Washington's large law firms have agreed to furnish twenty full-time lawyers a month to serve as defense counsel. Greene has also improved the performance of the regulars by incentive payments from government funds.

Other reforms proposed in the Subin report are being considered. The report recommended that plea bargaining, instead of being eliminated, should be formalized and made subject to full review by the trial judge (a recommendation also supported by the President's Crime Commission). This might lead to more trials, but the burden could be offset by the prosecutor's early elimination of unmerited charges. The practice of dropping charges against first offenders in return for good behavior—now used in a limited class of cases—would be expanded, avoiding the stigma of a criminal record. Conduct of prosecutors would be elevated by a serious training program for novices, and experienced men would be rotated back to General Sessions after a tour of duty in the District Court. As for the "Counter"—it has already been replaced by cubicles which permit hearings to be conducted in privacy.

One of the volume problems of the court was apparently resolved when the Court of Appeals ruled that chronic alcoholism can no longer be punished as a crime. This should have meant the elimination of many of the thirty thousand drunk cases that come to the court each year. The police nevertheless continued to arrest chronic alcoholics, only to have them released by the court. Chief Judge Greene called this practice "financially and psychologically wasteful." And he did not hesitate to condemn government bureaucrats who had failed to provide diagnostic and treatment facilities for alcoholics. Many of the men said they received better care before, when the alcoholic center was a prison, than now that it was called a "hospital."

Another answer to the court's volume problem looks more promising. Last year an office called the Citizens Information Service began operating in the basement of the courthouse. To this office, staffed by a lawyer and social workers, are referred many complaints formerly handled by prosecutors. People are directed to social agencies, where there is at least a chance their problems will be met. Creation of the Information Service was welcomed by Judge Tim Murphy, an outstanding new appointee. Said Murphy, who came to the bench after five years in the frustrating job of chief prosecutor: "I have always thought that the courts are the last place for people to come to in solving our social problems, not the first."

The great volume of business, Subin concludes from his study, is not the real problem. It is simply a symptom of society's failure to prevent these cases from reaching the courts. The lower courts have served as society's wastebasket. Into them have been thrown the unsolved problems and unmet grievances of the poor. The criminal court is not the only side of General Sessions. There is also a civil court, including a landlord-tenant branch, which orders thousands of summary evictions each year, and a small-claims court which functions mostly as a collection agency for retail stores and finance companies. In other words, the pattern of oppression of the poor is consistent throughout the court. The lower courts are part of the Other America, invisible to the rest of us, except perhaps on a forced visit to answer a traffic violation.

For traffic violators there is a powerful lobby to protest the injustices of the lower courts. Recently the AAA proposed the following reforms, as a bill of rights for traffic violators:

> The motorist should have to make only one appearance in court. His rights as a defendant should be clearly explained to him at the outset, and confusing court rules should be simplified. Courts must recognize the human frailty of a policeman's testimony, and give more sincere

attention to the motorist's side of the story. Courts must understand that some traffic-control devices are inadequate, some roads are improperly signed, and that unfair enforcement can exist. . . . Finally, it must be recognized that the motorist is not only innocent until proved otherwise, but also that he is a respectable, law-abiding citizen who has made an error, not a criminal. After all, he might be me. Or you.

For the respectable citizen there is a bill of rights—an understanding that cops lie, that there is unfair enforcement, that the defendant is presumed innocent, that he has not committed any crime but merely made an error. These reforms are necessary and they are good, but they are necessary and good for everyone. Until the respectable citizen understands that, there will be no justice for the People's Court.

8

Captives
of the
Crime War

The rituals surrounding the banishment of a law-breaker are very potent, but there are no rituals to remove from him the label of offender when he seeks to reenter the community.

—The Challenge of Crime in a Free Society,
REPORT OF THE PRESIDENT'S COMMISSION ON
LAW ENFORCEMENT AND ADMINISTRATION OF JUSTICE

On any one day there are nearly one-half million people confined in jails and prisons and another three-quarters of a million subject to other forms of correction. When the Crime Commission released these figures, based on a nationwide survey, it added that the number of persons restrained was so large that even experts in corrections were startled. The number is appalling, not because of the threat these persons pose to society, but because of the very absence of threat.

Most of the hundreds of thousands in local jails, detention homes, and reformatories are alcoholics, mental defectives, vagrants, or other misfits. American jails and prisons, the Crime Commission concluded, have become a "catch basin" for the human problems we have been unable to resolve. Even in penitentiaries, where most "serious" offenders are confined, the bulk of prisoners are serving time for nonviolent crimes. Generally the longest sentences are reserved for violent offenders, on the theory of deterrence. But the theory often doesn't fit the facts, since most violent crimes are committed impulsively against relatives or friends by men who are not professional criminals.

"For the bulk of offenders prison causes more problems than it solves." This conclusion of the Crime Commission is no surprise to prison officials, but it may come as a great surprise to members of the public. Life in many prisons, the Commission states, is "at best barren and futile, at worst unspeakably brutal and degrading." Prison conditions are one of the major obstacles to rehabilitation. In fact, psychiatrists believe the therapy most needed by ex-convicts is help to overcome the emotional scars of imprisonment. Yet if present trends in law enforcement continue—more and better police work and more efficient prosecution—there will be thousands and thousands of new candidates for our crime-generating prison system. Unless many of them can be diverted to a more effective route to correction, the cycle of imprisonment and crime will go on.

Imprisonment is really a new concept, not more than a few hundred years old. Before that, the accepted method for dealing with offenders (apart from banishment) was torture or execution, or both. A prison was a way station, a place to detain the offender until trial or carrying out of sentence. Since executions and torture were considered necessary to preserve public order, they took place in public view. Then man passed into a more civilized era; cruel methods gave way to "humanitarian" ones. Imprisonment was substituted for execution and torture, with the latter reserved for exceptional cases. The convict's lot was apparently improved, but some disagreed. George Bernard Shaw wrote in *The Crime of Imprisonment* that society eliminated plain torture because it could not tolerate the sense of guilt. But in its place, the prisoner was allowed to suffer conditions which were equally torturous. Only this time the torture was made invisible; prisons were put out of sight. What the public does not see, it

152

takes no responsibility for. People visit zoos and protest when they see animals mistreated. But no one—at least no one who counts—visits prisons.

Penologists try to make a distinction between *sentencing a man to prison* (which is his punishment) and *serving time* in prison (which is not supposed to be punishment). The distinction is patently dishonest. Living behind barbed wire and locked doors, under constant armed watch, with no privacy, no contacts with family, no normal sexual outlets—this is punishment no matter what label is attached to it. Shaw argued that society should go back to public torture; at least then its conscience might be prodded into taking responsibility for penal treatment. As an alternative, prisons—now conveniently isolated—should be thrown open to the public, and visiting encouraged.

Prison officials understand the job society has delegated to them. There are one hundred and twenty-one thousand persons employed in correction work, but only a small fraction deal with rehabilitation. The sole function of the rest is restraint and custody. In large state penitentiaries this makes some sense. Though most of the inmates are individually not dangerous, by herding them together in large numbers we create a dangerous situation. In small prisons, control can be maintained without rigid discipline, but the penitentiary is a pressure cooker which may blow its lid at any moment.

In *The Society of Captives* Gresham Sykes explains how the large maximum-security prison breeds violence. Guards impose harsh conditions on inmates to prevent potential disorder; this in turn increases the hostility of prisoners toward their captors. The prison official "is caught up in a vicious circle where he must suppress the very activity that he helps cause. It is not surprising . . .

that he should tend to view the prisoner as innately vicious or depraved. The conduct of the inmate is used to justify further repressive measures and the antagonisms between the guard and his prisoner spiral upward." For many inmates prison experience only reinforces their hatred of authority.

Part of the problem is money—money to tear down the monstrous fortresses we call penitentiaries, money to build a number of small minimum-security prisons and residential treatment centers. The Crime Commission says that since society has put prisons out of sight, they have had a low priority for public expenditures. But the Commission may be underestimating the resistance to prison reform. There is more involved than public indifference. In August, 1965, Myrl Alexander, Director of the Federal Bureau of Prisons, addressed an international conference on penology. To a group conscious that prison sentences in America are generally the longest in the world, Alexander said: "[P]unishment for the sake of punishment defeats the goals of society." Even while Alexander was condemning ill-treatment of prisoners, however, a majority of Americans questioned were telling a Gallup poll that the courts were not severe enough with convicted offenders.

Public opinion about crime, like opinion about everything else, is not made in a vacuum. Those inclined to take a hard line toward offenders are constantly fed ammunition from authoritative sources. Often the sources are law-enforcement officials. The late Police Chief William Parker of Los Angeles delivered periodic lectures about how soft the courts were on criminals. "Rehabilitation of the criminal [and] not the protection of society," Parker would say, has become the objective, as if the two were contradictory.

Whether the speaker is Chief Parker or J. Edgar Hoover,

the script is the same. Hoover has stated, for example: "We mollycoddle young criminals and release unreformed hoodlums to prey anew on society. The bleeding hearts, particularly among the judges, are so concerned for young criminals that they become indifferent to the rights of law-abiding citizens. . . ." After the Crime Commission reported that rehabilitation of offenders has not yet been given a fair trial, Hoover tried to undermine —if not repudiate—the Commission's findings. The Director wrote in one of his monthly messages "To All Law Enforcement Officials":

> Actually, the American public is seeking, and sorely needs, a proven formula to deter crime. The people are growing tired of substitutes. Swift detection and apprehension, prompt prosecution, and proper and certain punishment are tested crime deterrents.
>
> Coddling of criminals and soft justice increase crime; denials to the contrary have no valid support. Yet, these truths are still lost in the maze of sympathy and leniency heaped upon the criminal. Lame excuses and apologies offered for the lawbreaker are exceeded only by the amount of violence he commits.

The police tend to be a lobby for the enactment of harsher penal laws and the imposition of harsher sentences. With the exception of men like Parker and Hoover, policemen as individuals are not necessarily more punitive. Their toughness is an occupational attitude. When a long sentence is imposed in a case he investigated, it is taken as a measure of the importance of a policeman's work. Results in terms of conviction rate or the length of sentences mean not only more prestige for the individual cop but also more budgetary appropriations for the police agency. As a novice prosecutor, I once charged a defendant, arrested by the FBI for a crime within its statutory jurisdiction, with a treasury offense which he had also committed. Later I found out I had offended the Bureau by depriving it of credit for the arrest.

The Bureau has lobbied against an important reform in corrections policy known as "diversion before charge," or "deferred prosecution." Under this concept a first offender may avoid a conviction record by serving a short probationary period. If he performs satisfactorily during this period, the complaint against him is dropped. New York District Attorney Hogan has been following this practice for some time. In the federal system it is used for juveniles, but many in the Department of Justice would like to see it expanded to adult offenders. Their efforts have been stymied by the FBI's opposition. The real reason for the opposition: an increase in the number of nonconvictions would hurt the Bureau's precious "batting average."

Even such a moderate policeman as New York Commissioner Howard Leary is susceptible to the hard line. Though a partner in some enlightened experiments in criminal justice, Leary announced in early 1967 that the real way to stop crime was to enact harsher penalties, and he called for a complete review of New York's criminal laws. This prompted Professor Herbert Wechsler to respond: "This off-the-cuff opinon will, no doubt, be treated with the intelligent neglect that it deserves." Leary's ignorance came as a shock to Wechsler, who with other experts had been laboring for several years to revise New York's penal laws. If there was one change the revisers did not make, it was to increase criminal penalties.

One thing that disturbed Leary was that New York's multiple-offender laws, under which a "four-time loser" may be sentenced to life, were not being enforced. Prosecutors often allow three-time felons to plead guilty to a misdemeanor, instead of a felony, to avoid applying the mandatory life sentence. But this example does not help Leary's argument about sentencing; it does just the opposite. What the prosecutor is doing is to find an escape hatch from a cruel law, a law enacted during "crime-wave" hysteria in the twenties, when politicians responded to the same kind of pressure that prompted Leary to make his remarks.

The severity of the New York law was brought home to the public in 1930, when a woman who had shoplifted two dresses was sentenced to imprisonment for life. Her three previous felonies, committed over a period of ten years, involved the theft of a total of two dresses and two coats! On hearing herself sentenced to life, the defendant, not surprisingly, fainted. Later the judge, who had unwillingly pronounced sentence, stated publicly that he would take part in any movement that might bring a reduction in the woman's sentence.

In 1966, after ten years of abortive efforts, Congress finally pushed through a crime bill for the District of Columbia. It was a bill to delight the "get-tough" lobby. For example, a mandatory minimum sentence of twenty years was fixed for first-degree burglary, which is not even a crime of violence. President Johnson vetoed the bill as "a step backward in judicial and correction policy," adding that there was no need for such penalties in the District, where the sentences now being imposed are already among the highest in the country. Undeterred, Congress passed another District of Columbia Crime Bill at its next session with less severe though equally unwise mandatory minimum sentences.

The more affluent a man is, opinion polls show, the more punitive his attitude toward offenders. The rich have more to lose (though the poor are more often victims of crime than the rich). In the District of Columbia the strongest lobbies for harsh criminal statutes are the Board of Trade and an association of bankers. These groups take full-page ads in newspapers, write letters to the President, testify before Congress, and make speeches throughout the city—all to propagandize the need for more police powers, more rigid criminal laws, and more severe sentences.

These activities are reminiscent of the first citizens crime commission, which was formed in Chicago almost fifty years ago (see Chapter 1). One of the first projects of the Chicago Crime Commission was to keep a running box score of convicts sentenced to hang; each month the Commission's bulletin reminded the authorities of how many men were left unexecuted. Chicago was plagued by organized crime and gang warfare in the twenties, so that businessmen were not imagining the existence of crime. The trouble was that, like most alarmists, they exaggerated the threat, lumping the social misfits and defectives with professional gangsters. Taking a list of "murderers" which the Commission published, Clarence Darrow showed that only a few of the homicides involved premeditated killings or gang murders. In the same article, Darrow wrote:

> Readers of newspapers and periodicals are constantly regaled with lurid stories of crime. From time to time with great regularity these tales are pieced together to produce the impression that waves of crime are sweeping across the land. Long rows of figures generally go with these tales which purport to tabulate the number of murders, hold-ups, burglaries, etc., in given areas, and sometimes comparisons are drawn with other countries and with other periods. The general effect is always to

arouse anger and hatred, to induce legislatures to pass more severe laws, to fill the jails and penitentiaries, and to furnish more victims for the electric chair and gallows. It is a commonplace that cruel and hard punishments cannot be inflicted unless the populace is moved by hatred and fear. The psychology of fighting crime is the same as the psychology of fighting wars: the people must be made to hate before they will kill.

After the Chicago Crime Commission's first year in business, the crime rate appeared to decline, and the Commission patted itself on the back. But as soon as the rate climbed back up, the Commission looked for a scape-goat. It blamed soft-hearted judges and misguided social workers, with their "maudlin sympathy" for criminals. The favorite targets of the Commission were probation and parole, the only real advances in penology that had been made in centuries. Calling probation "a vicious measure," the president of the Commission demanded a return to old-fashioned retributive punishment, which had been effective in preserving life and property. "Our funda-mental criminal laws are the development of centuries of civilization," the Commission boasted, though it was dur-ing these centuries of civilization that a child could be hanged for stealing a loaf of bread or a stick of candy.

Even in the twenties it was customary for the vigilante groups to promote the myth that prisons were "country clubs." The Commission's president wrote: "If we are going to make Chicago a safe place to live in, one of the first things we must do is to provide punishment that punishes, instead of giving criminals a vacation in an institution where they have a better living than if they were free." Obviously the members of the Commission had never been inside the Cook County Jail, for two years later the Commission itself found that the jail was an archaic monstrosity where prisoners suffered from unbelievably filthy and overcrowded conditions.

Then, as now, indignant businessmen lobbied for tougher penalties. The theft of a car outraged them, and they tried to make every car theft punishable by a mandatory ten-year sentence. This proposal was rejected, but another Commission suggestion was adopted, fixing a minimum of one year and a maximum of twenty. Some convictions were obtained under this statute, but soon the public came to realize that most cars were taken by young boys on "joy rides." There was revulsion against the mandatory sentence. Prosecutors avoided using the statute, and when they did use it, judges and juries often refused to convict.

This backlash did not make the Crime Commission members happy. "Age must be forgotten and the matter treated as a menacing situation"; more thought should be given "to the feelings of the citizens who suffered at the hands of the car thief," ignoring that almost ninety percent of the cars were recovered shortly after they were taken. Without realizing it, the Crime Commission had become a front for the insurance companies, which wanted to keep their losses down. And inevitably the campaign of terror which the Commission mounted got out of control. Trigger-happy policemen killed several boys and seriously wounded others as they attempted to steal some cars. So the vigilantes had their way; the ultimate punishment had been inflicted for car theft.

Not all judges are bleeding hearts. Some share the vigilante mentality. In Philadelphia Judge Juanita Stout presides over the Juvenile Court with an iron hand and an overdose of moralism. Her views of criminology range from the idea that "there is no such thing as a 'joy ride'; theft is theft"—to the fear that we are in danger of turning the country over to "cheaters and 14-year-old illiterates armed with bicycle chains." Her views on social issues are in the same vein. She attacks the welfare system for subsidizing the lazy and immoral with taxpayers' money and advocates that mothers of more than two illegitimate children should be declared "unfit" and the children removed from the home. That these views meet with community approval is shown by the hundreds of favorable fan letters she gets each month. Judge Stout would probably be a likely candidate on a George Wallace ticket, were it not for the fact that she, like most of the alleged delinquents who appear in her court, is a Negro.

Judge Irving Kaufman, who sent the Rosenbergs to the electric chair, once described sentencing as an almost godlike function. This is true. But since the human beings who perform this function are less than godly, how can we ensure that they deal justly with offenders? At best there is lack of uniformity in the sentences imposed by different judges, at worst a bizarre disparity. In the same month recently two men were sentenced for cashing bad checks in a very small amount. Neither had a prior criminal record, and both of them cashed checks in time of great need due to family illness. The first man was sentenced to thirty days in jail; a different judge sentenced the second man to fifteen years in prison. On the same day in the same court in which Bobby Baker was sentenced to one to three years for income-tax evasion, larceny, and fraud, a twenty-four-year-old received the identical sentence for unauthorized use of a car.

One way to check such unfairness would be to give appellate courts power to reduce sentences on appeal—a power which they have in virtually every country except our own. Appellate judges are more removed from the vengeful climate of the crime war than trial judges and are thus less susceptible to community pressure. Appellate courts do not want to be charged with supervising the operation of lower courts, which is generally a sound principle. But sentencing is a crucial matter in which the restraint and perspective of upper courts is badly needed. Appellate judges already interfere with the sentencing process anyway. They do it indirectly, by reversing convictions, often in death cases, because of technical errors. This arouses unnecessary antagonism both in the lower courts and in the public. These decisions, which provide ammunition to punitive groups, could be avoided by a system of sentence review.

After its intensive study of corrections, the Crime Commission reached a striking conclusion—the real problem is not so much to correct the offender as to remake the attitudes of the community, to modify the resistance of the "good" citizen to the ex-convict. A community and its institutions always play a critical role in determining success or failure of the individual. Most offenders are already rejects from society. After they have been labeled as criminal and their ties broken by imprisonment, their sense of worthlessness is accentuated. If they are to avoid further crime, the Commission warns, they must be reconciled with the community.

The Crime Commission's conclusions parallel those of another government commission, which studied the mental-health problem several years ago. The theme of its report, *Action for Mental Health*, is that the disability associated with mental illness is largely imposed by rejection of the mental patient. An important cause of the disability is the mental hospital itself, with its "custodial culture," a culture created by public pressure for security. Only a radical change in public attitudes, the Commission felt, could bring about a return of the mental patient to the community, where rehabilitation could begin.

Too often in the past the community has deluded the offender, and itself, with the idea that corrections was a one-way street; iron out the kinks in the individual's personality, and he will turn out all right. But what good does it do to repair defects in the individual if opportunities are closed to him? Vocational training in prison, the Crime Commission points out, makes no sense if the ex-convict cannot get a job after his release.

"Sure, I found a job all right," an ex-offender told a panel of Washington citizens investigating local crime conditions. "Yeah, I found a job—in a Jiffy John." The panel did not ask for a further description. The point this makes—and that placement statistics hide—is that the jobs which most ex-offenders get are at lowest wages and poorest working conditions. As a result, few stay employed for long.

Prison administrators complain that they get shorted when it comes to spending public moneys. As long as there are no publicized prison riots or escapes, taxpayers do not care what goes on inside prisons. Despite this low priority, however, society ends up spending much more treating offenders in prison than it would spend treating them in the community. The cost of maintaining the average prisoner is more than ten times the cost of treating him on probation. Yet one-third of two hundred and fifty counties recently surveyed by the Crime Commission had no probation services at all. We do things the hard way because we seem to lack the sense, or foresight, to do them any other way.

The central question, the Crime Commission concluded,

is not *whether* to treat the offender in the community, but *how* to do so safely and successfully. The traditional means of handling transition from prison to civilian life is the parole system. A prisoner is released conditionally to the community to see whether he can adjust to ordinary life. Theoretically he has "paid his debt to society," but the disabilities he carries with him, other than his own personal defects, are enormous. The chief disability, of course, is his status as an ex-convict. Says James V. Bennett: "Returning prisoners are considered ineligible for public assistance, thought a security risk, hounded by the police and generally shunned and discriminated against wherever they turn. Is it any wonder that from forty to sixty per cent again revert to prison within five years?" Typically the prisoner is turned out into the street without funds. In his own state of Maryland, Bennett points out, "nothing is given a released prisoner to tide him over even the first day after one, three, five or twenty years in prison." Massachusetts is more generous, authorizing twenty-five dollars at discharge. But from this a prisoner must pay his own transportation home.

Release on parole is not automatic. Far from it. In most states the judge fixes only the minimum and maximum sentences—which may be many years apart. It is up to the parole board to decide when a man is ready to be released. The board members' discretion is absolute, and they often act with an arrogance to match their power. The prisoner must plead his case by himself. He has no advocate to object to unfair questions, no one to emphasize favorable features that his records might not show. The parole board is judge and jury and prosecutor. And there is no appeal from rejection of a parole application. The applicant must wait for another year, and perhaps another, going through the same painful process each time. The wise convict knows that the parole board is often made up of political hacks with no empathy for prisoners and that what they want to hear is a prisoner humble himself. He is the one most likely to be granted parole. But the man who can feign humility and go through the motions of self-chastisement may be underneath the most hostile to authority and the worst parole risk.

Parole conditions are ludicrous. The Chairman of the New York State Parole Board, Russell G. Oswald, has noted that a man can be returned to prison for drinking a glass of beer, meeting old friends (with criminal records), or seeing his girl friend in his room. "[I]n many instances," Oswald admitted, "we make these parolees lead a hell of a lot better life than we lead ourselves." This does not mean that strict conditions are all observed by parolees, nor that they are all enforced by undermanned parole departments. But it does mean that when an official wants to get a man returned to prison, he can always find some legal excuse for doing so.

The parole officer to whom the prisoner reports is supposed to act as a sort of social case worker, but this is in theory only. The Crime Commission found that parole officers are so pressed with an overload of cases and so concerned with trying to be policemen that they have little time to help on matters that count like finding jobs and solving family problems. Supervision usually consists of a ten- or fifteen-minute interview once or twice a month, in which the parole officer tells his charge to keep his nose clean. With all the talk of the danger that the convict presents to the community, and all the emphasis on security when he is in prison, the absence of parole supervision is incongruous.

An alternative to the parole system is "work release." Selected prisoners, whose terms are about to expire, are placed in jobs in the community and allowed out of the prison each day, to return at night. About half the states have adopted programs of this kind, and federal prisons are experimenting with work release under the 1965 Prisoner Rehabilitation Act. Several thousand federal inmates have already been employed under the Act. Their earnings, totaling hundreds of thousands of dollars, have been used to support their dependents, placed in savings accounts for use after release, or used for other purposes. Work release is the prisoner's opportunity to prove that he can "make it" on parole. One man wrote that he was trusted by his co-workers but that he "never forgot where [he] slept at night." The Rehabilitation Act is flexible enough to permit educational as well as work release. It allowed a federal inmate in Texas to be transferred to a prison in Michigan, near a town where his family had resettled. The prisoner traveled alone on a bus from Texas to Michigan. After his arrival, he enrolled in the University of Michigan to finish his education; each day he leaves the prison to attend classes at the university.

Only a small percentage of the federal work releasees have escaped; most of these had a history of alcoholism and a low threshold of resisting temptation. But the small number of failures is not necessarily meaningful. Men selected for the work release are the best "risks" to begin with, which is true of most experimental programs. Administrators are afraid of jeopardizing political and community support by failure. "We can't take any wild chances," Washington's Director of Corrections told a reporter. "Those guys on the Hill are watching us like a hawk. One construction worker hits his foreman on the head with a board, and the whole program is in trouble." A real test of the work-release idea must await the time when the program is expanded to include more questionable risks. Economic conditions in which work release is being tried are also favorable, and perhaps artificial. Officials admit that acceptance of prisoner workers is mostly due to a labor shortage. Any economic recession will be a severe setback to the program, for under the law it cannot operate in any area where there is a surplus of labor—a further indication of the tenuous support for prisoner rehabilitation.

The disability of a criminal record applies not only to ex-convicts but also to persons who have been arrested and had charges against them dismissed. Though a decent job is recognized as indispensable to rehabilitation, most job opportunities are closed to men with a criminal record. Hiring resistance is not confined to private employers. About half the states and municipalities admit that they never employ ex-offenders. If public employers take this attitude, private ones can hardly be expected to do otherwise. Not long ago the OEO had to defend a congressional attack on the hiring of ex-offenders by community action programs. "It might be shocking to some people," an OEO executive said, "but it's a plain fact that the tough youths will respect the former criminal who tells them about his experience and warns them about repeating it."

Recognizing that it should set an example in employment of ex-offenders, the federal government is revising its own policies. The Civil Service Commission no longer requires that arrests be listed on federal job applications, and even convictions may be omitted if the offender was under twenty-one. Still, there is a certain deception about these reforms. The authorities will continue to investigate prospective employees, will look for gaps in employment history, and may even resort to local police files for criminal records. And as such information becomes increasingly computerized, the likelihood of discovering scars in an employee's past will be greatly expanded. This comes back again to the point that rehabilitation cannot depend on secrecy or nondisclosure but must be based on conscious acceptance of the ex-offender by the rest of the community.

It would be a mistake to discount all resistance to ex-offenders as an act of pathology. Some of it is based upon honest fear. There are vicious incorrigibles as well as some compulsive offenders who easily lose control, and society is entitled to be protected from them. To place a child molester in a job dealing with children, for example, is a risk greater than a community can be expected to tolerate. The problem is in defining the risk, in understanding the particular dangers involved in rehabilitating particular individuals. It is here that our judgments tend to be irrational. We lump all ex-offenders together, without distinguishing between the small minority that are dangerous and the large majority that are not, or between those that present a general danger and those that present only a specific risk. Through such indiscriminate lumping, the majority of ex-offenders are dragged down to the level of the most vicious criminal.

If the Crime Commission report teaches us anything, it is that many crimes are not reported and many criminals not detected. If many criminals are not caught, why assume that those we do catch are the most dangerous? In one sense the probability goes the other way: the most intelligent and devious offenders may be the ones most likely to avoid detection. The community is outraged whenever a prisoner escapes from confinement; alarms are broadcast and doors locked. Yet without knowing it we probably rub shoulders every day with men far more dangerous.

How much danger is society capable of tolerating? Not

very much, if one is to judge by the fear and rejection of ex-offenders. To give them a second chance involves risks. But *not* to give them a second chance may involve risks, too. The wish for absolute security, the intolerance of danger, has its own dangers. A society obsessed with security, incapable of giving up enough of it to make peace with its rebels and deviants, is a society which is asking for trouble.

9

Sour Note on the Trumpet

We must be careful not to underestimate the violence of the public's feelings of vengeance and desire to fix blame. What we are trying to do is to change the rules of war, and that is not done lightly. We think highly of due process because we want to keep inviolate our right to take an eye for an eye: revenge protected by rules of fair play amounts to holy war.

—Judge Curtis Bok

9

Some More on the Trumpet

In 1963 the Supreme Court decided the case of *Gideon* v. *Wainwright,* establishing that every man charged with a serious crime has a right to a lawyer to defend him. The *Gideon* case, according to then Attorney General Kennedy, showed that "the very survival of our belief in democratic justice" depended on preserving the adversary system. When Gideon was tried without a lawyer, he was convicted and sent to prison for five years. When a lawyer was appointed to defend him, Gideon was acquitted. The syllogism was perfect. Lawyers are indispensable. The *Gideon* case enhanced the public image of the American lawyer and Anthony Lewis' best-selling book, *Gideon's Trumpet,* made the defendant into a national folk hero. But the rosy picture of American justice, and its adversary system, which the *Gideon* case conveyed was not the complete picture. The case left unanswered some serious questions about the continued utility of the adversary system, the reasons it has resisted change, and questions about the bar's ability to meet current needs of criminal justice, which have little relationship to traditional advocacy.

After the *Gideon* case the adversary system received another boost as a result of the Oswald case. Unresolved doubts about the assassination were attributed to a failure to bring Oswald to trial. The Warren Commission wrote:

> If Oswald had lived he could have had a trial by American standards of justice where he would have been able to exercise his full rights under the law. A judge and jury would have presumed him innocent until proven guilty beyond a reasonable doubt. He might have furnished information which could have affected the course of his trial. He could have participated in and guided his defense. There could have been an examination to determine whether he was sane under prevailing legal standards. All witnesses, including possibly the defendant, could have been subject to searching examination under the adversary system of American trials.

Although the Commission rejected the idea of conducting its inquiry according to an adversary model, it found it difficult to resist its influence. A few months after the inquiry started, the Commission yielded to pressure and appointed a lawyer to look out for Oswald's interests. But the appointment was more calculated for its effect on public relations than on actual conduct of the investigation. The lawyer appointed—Walter Craig, President of the American Bar Association—had almost no experience in criminal defense.

Craig was merely charged with advising the Commission whether the "proceedings conformed to the basic principles of American justice." It was a halfhearted compromise which did not satisfy the critics. For example, Yale Professor Eugene Rostow, while praising the Warren report generally, regretted that Craig "was not the lawyer for Oswald and his family" and that "public hearings analogous to those of a trial were not held." Rostow's support for the adversary system went not just to methods of developing evidence but also to the cathartic effect which a jury trial is supposed to have, tending to resolve any public doubts about the result.

But while an adversary trial may assuage the public conscience, it does not necessarily put an end to speculation about the defendant's guilt, particularly in a political trial, as the Sacco-Vanzetti, Rosenberg, and other cases demonstrate. Besides, the notion that an adversary trial is a more effective means of developing truth than a commission inquiry is unsound. Had Oswald lived to be tried, there is nothing to suggest that the prosecutor would have done any better with the ballistics evidence than the Commission did, and it is far-fetched to think that Oswald's defenders would have had an interest in suggesting he was only one of several assassins. It is common for the adversary system to produce this kind of "stand-off," when fear of incriminating himself stops a defendant from exposing error in prosecution evidence.

It is ironic that the Oswald case has become a rallying point for faith in the adversary system. Not long ago the ABA reported that the adversary system was the chief obstacle to educating the public about a lawyer's "professional responsibility." It found that the bar could not respond to the charge that a lawyer is "nothing but a hired brain and voice," a "mouthpiece." Even law students, the ABA said, are "uneasy about the adversary system, some thinking of it as an unwholesome compromise with the combativeness of human nature. . . ." The system actually has its origin in combat. It goes back to the days when disputes were settled by contest between champions for each side. Adversary is simply a euphemism for enemy. The present-day trial is also an out-growth of the physical ordeals by which truth was tested in criminal cases. In the ordeal by water, for example, the suspect was thrown into the sea. If he survived, he was innocent; if not, he was guilty. A modern defendant in a spectacular trial goes through a similar experience in facing an ordeal by publicity.

The adversary trial had a particular appeal for nineteenth-century America, as a relief from the monotony of rural existence. Roscoe Pound describes the American tendency to make the criminal trial a spectacle, a "circus," as in Roman times. "During 'court week' the wagons of the farmers were tied up about the court house square and an appreciative audience watched the fine points of the trial-game as an urban audience might watch the fine points of a professional baseball game."

Recalling his early career as a country lawyer in Ohio, Clarence Darrow wrote that lawsuits were filled with color, life, and wit. The populace took sides "and entire communities were divided as if in war." In most primitive societies the function of law—including criminal law—is to help parties adjust, to make peace among neighbors. In contrast, Darrow wrote that the country "show" trial "left in its wake a chain of hatreds and scars that never healed."

The example of the Ruby trial should be an answer to arguments that a trial of Oswald would have revealed the truth about the assassination. The Ruby trial shows up as a caricature of the adversary system. Sybille Bedford, the noted British court reporter, thought she was witnessing a "blood-and-thunder" spectacle straight out of the nineteenth century. Most of the distortions in fact-finding which trials like this produce come about because the participants use the trial as a vehicle for self-exposure. The defendant becomes a pawn in the game between contending lawyers.

Much of the hatred generated in the Ruby trial, wrote Melvin Belli after Jack Ruby's conviction, "tended to focus upon me, the direct challenger of the Dallas oligarchy and the Dallas image. Our adversary system of justice tends to put the spotlight on the lawyers rather than on the poor creature who is on trial. . . ." What attracted Belli to the Ruby case was the hope of remaking the rules of legal insanity and thus expanding his own reputation in forensic medicine. Belli insisted, however, that his "main cause was the attempt to save the life of this one lonely man."

Few people in Dallas predicted a death penalty in the case, and, in fact, most of the "Dallas oligarchy" was shocked when the jury returned its verdict. On the other hand, no one familiar with the mood of Dallas—certainly no psychologist as astute as Belli—could miss the fact that the jury could not let Ruby get away with murder entirely. His acquittal would have fed the image of frontier justice which Dallas had already conveyed to the world. Yet Belli deliberately refrained from asking for mercy, as if to challenge the jury to return a death verdict. This was a grandstand play, an act of indifference to the client whose life he was supposedly intent on saving.

After the verdict came in, Belli berated the jury, the judge, and the people of Dallas. He told reporters that he and his law associates in the case were "crying," crying for "our profession and for justice." In his book about the trial, Belli refers to "all that happened [in Dallas] to me," and finally adds, almost as an afterthought: "and to my client Jack Ruby."

After the trial, Ruby's family fired Belli and looked

around for a less publicity-conscious lawyer to handle the appeal. At one point they negotiated with Percy Foreman of Houston, but Foreman would not approve the no-publicity policy. He wrote to Ruby: "You were tried and convicted in the news media before you were in court. Both convictions ought to be set aside. Change in public opinion may help bring about a reversal in the appellate courts." It was later reported that one of the terms Foreman tried to get from Ruby's family was a percentage of income from exploitation of Ruby's life story in various media. The appeal was finally handled by a team of lawyers who scrupulously observed the family's policy. Relying strictly on legal arguments—one of which attacked handling of publicity during the trial itself—the lawyers convinced the appellate court to reverse Ruby's conviction.

Foreman probably was not bothered by losing a chance to represent Ruby. He is in constant demand in murder trials, where he commands huge fees and displays a classic adversary lawyer's ability to obfuscate the truth. "The best defense in a murder trial," Foreman says, "is the fact that the deceased should have been killed, regardless of how it happened." In the Candy Mossler trial he followed his own advice. His opening to the jury was a tirade against the murdered man, promising evidence that Mossler had "every conceivable sex deviation that anybody has ever had. . . ." It is no surprise to learn that such evidence was never produced. There was evidence, however, that local police had picked up a man wandering around in a bruised state on the night of the murder, obviously after a fight. Foreman let the jury know that the man was "queer," implying that he, and not Foreman's client, murdered Mossler. After his client was acquitted, Foreman admitted to the press that he never really believed his own story.

One might almost say, writes Professor Harold Lasswell, that a lawyer functions without values. "The usual training leaves him believing that he has no opportunities or responsibilities other than to serve his clients by whatever means are not forbidden. And he moves in a world of perpetual self-congratulation in which the glories of the law and hence of the lawyer are suitable topics of declamation wherever the members of the bar are ceremonially assembled."

The *Gideon* case has caused much self-congratulation. Clarence Earl Gideon was a Florida prisoner who took his burglary conviction to the highest court, in the belief that he had been entitled to a lawyer at his trial. Under the law existing at that time he was not, but now the Supreme Court vindicated Gideon's judgment. In a unanimous opinion, the Court ruled that Florida had to give Gideon the free services of a lawyer and sent the case back for retrial, where Gideon was assigned an experienced local lawyer to defend him. The second trial offers some insight into the operation of the adversary system.

When the case was before the Supreme Court, Gideon had written to attorney (now Justice) Abe Fortas, who argued his appeal: "I always believed that the primarily [sic] reason of trial in a court of law was to reach the truth. My trial was far from the truth," he added. At the first trial Gideon did little to shake the testimony of the state's main witness, Henry Cook, who claimed he saw Gideon inside the Bay Harbor Poolroom at five-thirty A.M. on the morning it was burglarized. At the second trial, the strategy of appointed counsel Fred Turner was to charge the burglary to Cook himself. He insinuated that Cook was trying to absolve himself by implicating Gideon, although Gideon's own theory was that the owner of the poolroom may have framed him.

THE CRIME WAR

No one can be sure what went on inside the jury room that led to Gideon's acquittal. Perhaps Turner's strategy of pinning the burglary on Cook was decisive. Perhaps it was that Gideon had already spent two years in prison, a fact brought out at the trial. Whatever the reason, the acquittal did not prove Gideon's innocence, but simply that the jurors did not believe him guilty beyond a reasonable doubt.

Laymen often assume that the goal of a criminal trial is truth, as Gideon did in his letter to Fortas, and that an acquittal means innocence. But there are special rules that govern a criminal trial. Each juror must believe the defendant guilty beyond a reasonable doubt. If plain truth were the goal, the judge would simply tell the jurors to convict if they believed the state's evidence, as in civil cases. But the reasonable-doubt test prevents conviction without a high degree of certainty. This is often expressed in the saying that it is better to let ten guilty men escape than to convict one innocent one.

To a defense attorney, whether or not his client is guilty is for most purposes irrelevant. Even if Gideon were guilty of the poolroom burglary, Fred Turner could properly defend him at the trial. Since an accused is presumed to be innocent, his lawyer has the right to sit back and make the state prove its case. But Turner did more than that. His strategy was to pin the burglary on Cook. This he could not have ethically done if he knew his client was guilty. This is where the gamelike nature of the adversary trial becomes clear.

How does a lawyer "know" when his client is guilty? Normally he knows if the client has admitted guilt to him. But suppose there has been no admission, yet from all the evidence the lawyer "believes" his client to be guilty. According to the canons of ethics, a mere "personal opinion" of guilt does not amount to knowledge. Since knowledge is a disability, there is a premium on remaining ignorant. Usually this is easy, for guilty defendants almost invariably lie to their lawyers—at least at first. With a strong instinct for self-preservation, they sense that a disenchanted lawyer might not defend the case very vigorously. When lawyer and client know the ground rules, they carefully avoid a full airing of the facts. The lawyer's preparation of his case is hardly a search for truth, for in most cases truth is the very thing which would send his client to the penitentiary.

If the defendant is a novice and does not know the ground rules, he may say too much or not use the right words, and it may be necessary for the lawyer to rewrite his story. In *Anatomy of a Murder,* after hearing his client's account of the crime, the defense lawyer responds:

> If the facts are as you have stated them so far, you have no defense, and you will very likely be electrocuted. On the other hand if you acted in a blind rage, there is a possibility of saving your life. Think it over, and we will talk about it tomorrow.

The late Judge Jerome Frank was the leading critic of the adversary system. He writes in *Courts on Trial* that the partisanship of opposing lawyers can block out or distort vital evidence, that honest witnesses are bewildered and made to look ridiculous by misleading cross-examination. "The lawyer considers it his duty to create a false impression . . . of any witness who gives [unfavorable] testimony." This type of advocacy is not confined to defense lawyers. In the *Berger* opinion thirty years ago, the Supreme Court set the ethical standard that a prosecutor's duty is "not to convict but to see that justice is done." The opinion was provoked by a young prosecutor's excess of adversary zeal in winning a conviction:

> He was guilty of misstating the facts in his cross-examination of witnesses; of putting into the mouths of such witnesses things which they had not said; of suggesting by his questions that statements had been made to him personally out of court, in respect of which no proof was offered; of pretending to understand that a witness had said something which he had not said and persistently cross-examining the witness on that basis; of assuming prejudicial facts not in evidence; of bullying and arguing with witnesses. . . .

The tactics which the Court condemned, with some changes in verbiage, can regrettably be found in almost any standard manual of courtroom tactics. The most ironic thing about the opinion, however, is that the young prosecutor whose conduct was condemned is today one of the country's leading defense "mouthpieces."

Lawyers hate to be reminded that they are mouthpieces. Sometimes an outspoken lawyer makes himself professionally unpopular by speaking the truth. The most celebrated debate on the ethics of advocacy took place between a distinguished Boston lawyer, Charles P. Curtis, and the Chairman of the Bar Association's Ethics Committee, Henry Drinker. "There is nothing unethical in . . . advocating what you don't believe in," Curtis wrote in a law review. "We are not dealing with the morals which govern a man acting for himself, but with the ethics of advocacy. . . . I don't know any other career that offers ampler opportunity for both the enjoyment of virtue and the exercise of vice, or, if you please, the exercise of virtue and the enjoyment of vice, except possibly the ancient rituals which were performed in some temples by vestal virgins, in others by sacred prostitutes." An indignant Mr. Drinker replied to this "insidious essay," which would give law students and young lawyers "so many distorted and misleading" notions about lawyers' duties.

There is a narrow area in which the adversary system makes a useful contribution. This is the opportunity it gives to dramatize issues which need to be brought before the public. Yet when Robert Kennedy equated the adversary system with the survival of democracy, he overstated the case. So did his committee on law and poverty (1963): "The survival of our system of criminal justice and the values which it advances depends upon a constant, searching, and creative questioning of official decisions and assertions of authority at all stages of the process." This promises more than the adversary system can deliver. The "assertions of authority" which are challenged tend to be those from the lowest level of power—the police. Rarely are the more dangerous political abuses of power challenged in the courts. These abuses are immune from legal attack because they are institutionalized. Except for a few lawyers like Charles Morgan of Atlanta, the civil-liberties movement and the adversary system function largely as harmless irritants—outlets for anti-authoritarian impulses, which do not really threaten authority itself.

The American Civil Liberties Union's entry into the *Gideon* case, for example, can hardly be put in the category of defense of unpopular causes. It was clear from the moment that the Supreme Court granted certiorari—on a petition handwritten by Gideon in prison—that the Court would reverse the conviction and overrule its earlier right-to-counsel decisions.

From the Florida court, where Gideon was "railroaded" to a five-year prison term, to the Supreme Court, where his constitutional rights were vindicated, the balance of power between the state and the accused was radically reversed. After the right to appeal was granted, the legal establishment rallied to the defendant's side. Representing Gideon was one of America's ablest lawyers, Abe Fortas, and his high-powered Washington law firm, with supporting arguments by former Solicitor General J. Lee Rankin and a staff of law professors appearing for the ACLU. In addition, a group of professors from Harvard Law School filed a brief on behalf of twenty-three states which already recognized the right to trial counsel. Gideon's conviction was unanimously reversed.

I do not discount the symbolic importance of the *Gideon* case. We have come a long way since the seventeenth and eighteenth centuries, when torture was the favorite means of eliciting truth and defense lawyers were considered an obstruction. It is only a century or so since England permitted lawyers in felony cases. Before that time a man charged with a petty crime was entitled to a lawyer; but not one whose life was at stake. The lawyer was welcome where the consequences were least significant. Yet as far as we have come in the protection of human rights, the anomalies of American justice parallel those in early England.

Civil libertarians are preoccupied by nightmares like the Inquisition but almost indifferent to the fate of men ground down not by torture but by impersonal forces like mass-production justice (see Chapter 7). Americans are a sentimental people. Sometimes hypocritically so. We dramatize the case of the innocent man convicted while ignoring the mass of admitted offenders who are herded like cattle through the judicial and penal system. As for lawyers, they like the adversary system because it offers an opportunity to dramatize themselves—sometimes at the expense of their clients. But there is an urgent need for the use of advocacy in a less dramatic context, for championing rights of a different nature.

Most defendants hardly get a taste of the adversary system—eighty percent of them plead guilty. The informal procedures by which they are disposed of contrast sharply to the elaborate network of rules that govern the adversary trial. Many convicted men are sentenced to prison terms without lawyers to argue for mitigation, or with a lawyer so poorly informed of his client's background that he can make no intelligent argument. If there is abdication of advocacy at this stage, once sentence has been imposed the doors of the adversary system really slam shut. Prison officials and parole boards who take over brook no interference from lawyers, assuming any tried to become involved. Absence of the adversary system at this end of the process is an anomaly, since for most defendants the only issue in their case is how long they will serve in prison. By releasing a convict on parole after a minimum time served, or denying or revoking parole, correctional authorities can exercise total control over a man's life. With no one to protect the prisoner's rights, it is no surprise to find bizarre abuses, like revoking a man's parole—and imposing an unexpired twenty-four-year term —for attending his sister's funeral without written permission.

This is the real world of criminal justice, not the world in which the Percy Foremans and the Melvin Bellis move and make large fees, or the world in which professional libertarians vindicate great rights. Clarence Gideon's own history shows how experience in this real world can shape a man into a chronic offender.

Gideon's family were factory workers in Missouri. He was strictly disciplined by his mother and stepfather, who were highly moralistic churchgoers. At fourteen he ran away and lived with a relative in California, but his mother had him brought back and put in a detention home. Later he escaped and burglarized a clothing store, which brought him under the jurisdiction of the juvenile court. His mother asked the judge to send him away to the reformatory, which was done. "Of all the *prisons* I have been in," Gideon later wrote to his lawyer, Abe Fortas, "that was the worst." Gideon claimed he was still carrying scars from the whippings he received there.

After a year in the reformatory he was paroled, but he could not find steady employment. Two years later, at eighteen, he was convicted of robbery and sentenced to ten years in the Missouri penitentiary. Released on parole after four years, Gideon came out to a depression-ridden country in which it was almost impossible to find a job. Two years later he was back in prison—this time for theft from a government armory. He was then only twenty-four.

In prison he worked in a shoe factory and made enough money to send some home to his parents. He was released in 1937 after serving two years and managed to remain out of prison for two more years. Then he was charged with burglary, convicted as a second-felony offender, and sentenced to ten years. He escaped from prison in 1943 and worked under an alias as a railroad brakeman for one year; then he was caught and returned to prison for six more years.

In 1950 he was released from prison. Now forty years old, he entered into the first of three unsuccessful marriages. One year later he was back in prison, this time in Texas. He served another year and after release did odd jobs and gambled. Then he contracted tuberculosis and had part of a lung removed, remaining in a government hospital for eighteen months. When he married for the third time, it was to a woman with three children, who later bore three of his own children. In 1957 he decided to leave Texas "because my personal record was holding me down." He came to Panama City, Florida, in search of a new life, but his record followed him. He was arrested and jailed twice on charges that did not stick.

During one of these periods in jail the Welfare Department obtained custody of his children because his wife was drinking. He later managed to get the children back but received neither help nor money from welfare, apparently because of his criminal record. "In desperation," he turned to the Baptist Church. "I class that organization in the same class as I do the K.K.K.," he said, "because they hate too many persons and things. . . ." But he thought this was his only hope for making his children "respectable." After a long stretch in the hospital for treatment of TB, he left Florida for Baton Rouge, Louisiana, where he worked and sent his wife twenty dollars a week. Then he found out that the Juvenile Court had taken custody of the children again and returned to Panama City and tried to make a living gambling. Soon after, he was charged with burglarizing the poolroom and convicted. In the light of this history, one might conclude that whether or not Gideon was guilty of the burglary is almost irrelevant.

It is no surprise that nothing changed much for Gideon after his case was over. A year after the second trial, he was interviewed by a reporter, who wrote that he was "about as destitute as before. A lonely man, he ships out of Panama City occasionally on a fishing boat but is otherwise idle." On May 14, 1965, on one of the back pages of *The New York Times* there appeared a brief news item datelined Louisville, Kentucky. Clarence Earl Gideon had been arrested for vagrancy by local police. He was passing through the city, looking for a job but unable to find one. He pleaded guilty to the vagrancy charge and was released, after telling the judge that he would head for St. Louis and try to find work there.

Gideon's history, as depressing as it is, is not unusual. There are thousands of Gideons trudging through the courts and the prisons in a perpetual revolving door—men we stigmatize so they cannot get a job and then treat their unemployment as a crime. In Gideon's case it is not difficult to see how the cycle began, with his first brutalizing contact with the criminal justice system—the juvenile reformatory, the worst "prison" he was ever in.

Justice Abe Fortas must have been thinking of his former client when the case of fifteen-year-old Gerald Gault came before him in 1967. Gerald had been committed to the Arizona Industrial School for making obscene telephone calls to a woman. Once such a school acquires jurisdiction over a child, he may be detained until his twenty-first birthday. The parents of the boy complained that he had been railroaded to the reformatory, without a trial or a lawyer or a chance to face his accusers. He did not even have a transcript of the juvenile-court hearing so that an appeal could be taken. The Arizona Supreme Court had replied to the latter argument that "the evidence adduced at a juvenile hearing is of a confidential nature . . ." and that there was no appeal from a juvenile commitment anyway. The Court justified the nonadversary character of juvenile-court proceedings:

> [J]uvenile courts do not exist to punish children for their transgressions against society. The juvenile court stands in the position of a protecting parent rather than a prosecutor. It is an effort to substitute protection and guidance for punishment, to withdraw the child from

188

criminal jurisdiction and use social sciences regarding the study of human behaviour which permit flexibilities within the procedures. The aim of the court is to provide individualized justice for children. . . . The delinquent is the child of, rather than the enemy of society and their interests coincide.

High motives and enlightened impulses, said Justice Fortas in reversing Gerald Gault's conviction, but "juvenile court history has again demonstrated that unbridled discretion, however benevolently motivated, is frequently a poor substitute for principle and procedure." The "condition of being a boy," Fortas added, "does not justify a kangaroo court. . . . The essential difference between Gerald's case and a normal criminal case is that safeguards available to adults were discarded in Gerald's case. The summary procedure as well as the long commitment were possible because Gerald was 15 years of age instead of over 18." For an adult the maximum punishment for making an obscene telephone call would be a fine of five to fifty dollars or imprisonment for not more than two months, while Gerald Gault was committed for a possible maximum of six years!

The Gault case is an answer to some critics of the adversary system, who would replace adversary procedures entirely by the humanitarian and scientific approach. This is the approach of Soviet Justice, in which adult courts are modeled on the juvenile-court system and the judge, acting as a parent or teacher, deals with "the whole man" in an effort to remake him. The informality of Soviet justice may be a welcome relief from some of our archaic traditions, but its grinding and oppressive quality is reflected in such features as the harsh sentence imposed in the name of "rehabilitation."

THE CRIME WAR

In an ideal world, perhaps the humanitarian concept might work. But "teacher" or "parent" who knows what's best for the offender is a role filled by a human being, often an imperfect one. Justice Fortas recognized this in his opinion when he noted that half the juvenile-court judges had no college degree, one-fifth had never been to college at all, and one-fifth were not even lawyers.

The answer is not to eliminate due process and turn the system over to the "experts." The answer is not to get rid of lawyers but to put them in different places. America is facing a crisis in distribution—not simply of material goods but also of human and legal rights. We have inflated the importance of due process in a limited class of cases, while neglecting the massive needs of others. What is needed is a radical revision of social priorities. There is something terribly wrong with a system which shows a humane facade, while it sweeps its ugly problems under the rug—which in the juvenile court, for example, "saves" people from punishment by finding them "delinquent" and then commits them to institutions where there are no facilities to treat them; a system which gets a defendant "off" only to send him back into the revolving door of despair. This is the sour note on Gideon's trumpet.

Selected
Bibliography

CHAPTER 1

BOOKS

Bell, Daniel. *The End of Ideology.* New York: Macmillan, 1958. Also New York: The Free Press.
Clark, Kenneth B. *Dark Ghetto.* New York: Harper & Row, 1965.
Cloward, Richard A., and Ohlin, Lloyd E. *Delinquency and Opportunity.* New York: The Free Press, 1960, also 1966.
Comfort, Alex. *Authority and Delinquency in the Modern State.* London: Routledge & Kegan Paul, 1950.
Cook, Fred. J. *The FBI Nobody Knows.* New York: Macmillan, 1964. Also New York: Pyramid Books.
Harrington, Michael. *The Other America.* New York: Macmillan, 1962. Also Baltimore: Penguin Books.
Hofstadter, Richard. *The Paranoid Style in American Politics.* New York: Knopf, 1965.
Kennedy, Robert F. *The Pursuit of Justice,* Ch. 10. New York: Harper & Row, 1964.
Lowenthal, Max. *The Federal Bureau of Investigation.* New York: Sloane Associates, 1950.
Reiwald, Paul. *Society and Its Criminals.* New York: International Universities Press, 1950.
Steffens, Lincoln. *Autobiography,* Ch. XIV. New York: Harcourt, Brace & Company, Inc., 1936.
Waskow, Arthur I. *From Race Riot to Sit-in.* New York: Doubleday, 1966.
White, Theodore H. *The Making of a President, 1964.* New York: Atheneum, 1965.
Whyte, William F. *Street Corner Society.* Chicago: University of Chicago Press, 1943.

ARTICLES

Beattie, Ronald H. "Criminal Statistics in the United States–1960," *Journal of Criminal Law, Criminology and Police Science,* Vol. 51, p. 49 (1960).
Biderman, Albert D. "Social Indicators and Goals," in Bauer, Raymond A. *Social Indicators* (Cambridge: M.I.T. Press, 1966).
Darrow, Clarence. "Crime and the Alarmists," *Harper's,* Vol. 153, p. 535 (1926).

Selected Bibliography

Fulbright, J. W. "The Great Society Is a Sick Society," *New York Times Magazine*, August 20, 1967, p. 20.

Geis, Gilbert. "Crime and Politics," *The Nation*, August 14, 1967, p. 115.

Kamisar, Yale. "When the Cops Were not 'Handcuffed,'" *New York Times Magazine*, November 7, 1965, p. 34.

Lejins, Peter P. "Uniform Crime Reports," *Michigan Law Review*, Vol. 64, p. 1011 (1966).

Mackenzie, John P. "The Compromise Report on Crime," *The New Republic*, February 4, 1967, p. 15.

Marine, Gene. "I've Got Nothing Against the Colored, Understand," *Ramparts*, November 1966, p. 13.

Nixon, Richard M. "What Has Happened to America?" *Reader's Digest*, October 1967, p. 49.

Remington, Frank. "The Challenge of Crime," *The New Republic*, May 20, 1967, p. 38.

Ridgeway, James. "Barry Fights Crime," *The New Republic*, October 3, 1964, p. 9.

Robison, Sophia M. "A Critical View of the Uniform Crime Reports," *Michigan Law Review*, Vol. 64, p. 1031 (1966).

Wechsler, Herbert. "A Caveat on Crime Control," *Journal of Criminal Law and Criminology*, Vol. 27, p. 629 (1937).

Westley, William A. "The Escalation of Violence through Legitimation," *Annals*, Vol. 364, p. 120 (1966).

Wolfgang, Marvin E. "Uniform Crime Reports: A Critical Appraisal," *University of Pennsylvania Law Review*, Vol. 111, p. 708 (1963).

Wright, J. Skelly. "Crime in the Streets and The New McCarthyism," *The New Republic*, October 9, 1965, p. 10.

REPORTS AND STUDIES

Chicago Crime Commission, *Bulletins* (1919–1923).

Hoover, J. Edgar, Director, FBI. *Crime in the United States—Uniform Crime Reports* (Annual).

National Commission on Law Observance and Enforcement, *Report on Criminal Statistics* (1931).

President's Commission on Law Enforcement and Administration of Justice, *The Challenge of Crime in a Free Society*, Washington, D.C., U.S.G.P.O., 1967.

President's Commission on Law Enforcement and Administration of Justice, *Task Force Reports: Assessment of Crime, Juvenile Delinquency and Youth Crime, The Police*, Washington, D.C., U.S.G.P.O., 1967.

President's Commission on Law Enforcement and Administration of Justice, *Field Surveys I: Report on a Pilot Study in the District of Columbia on Victimization and Attitudes Toward Law Enforcement*, prepared by The Bureau of Social Science Research, Washington, D.C., U.S.G.P.O., 1967.

Report of the President's Commission on Crime in the District of Columbia, Washington, D.C., U.S.G.P.O., 1966.

MISCELLANEOUS

Johnson, Lyndon B., President. "Crime in America," Message to Congress, February 6, 1967.

Johnson, Lyndon B., President. Message on Veto of Omnibus Crime Bill for the District of Columbia, November 13, 1966.

Johnson, Lyndon B., President. "Crime, Its Prevalence, and Measures of Prevention," Message to Congress, March 8, 1965.

Law Enforcement and Criminal Justice Assistance Act of 1967 (submitted as Safe Streets and Crime Control Act of 1967) H.R. 5037, 90th Congress, 1st Session.

Republican Coordinating Committee, Statement on Riots, July 24, 1967.

Katzenbach, Nicholas DeB., Attorney General. Speech to the American Jewish Committee, November 11, 1965.

Kennedy, Robert F., Attorney General. Speech to American Bar Association Section on Criminal Law, August 10, 1964.

Meet the Press, February 19, 1967, National Broadcasting Co.

Omnibus Crime Bill for the District of Columbia, Public Law 90–226 (1967).

United States Senate, Subcommittee on Criminal Law and Procedures of the Committee on the Judiciary, Hearings on [Various] Crime Bills, March 22–24 and May 10–11, 1966, 89th Congress, 2d Session.

United States Senate, Committee on the Judiciary, Hearings on the Nomination of Thurgood Marshall as Justice of the Supreme Court of the United States, July 13–14, 1967, 90th Congress, 1st Session.

CHAPTER 2

BOOKS

Becker, Howard S. *Outsiders*. New York: The Free Press, 1963, also 1966.

Feifer, George. *Justice in Moscow*. New York: Simon & Schuster, 1964. Also New York: Delta-Dell.

Gerassi, John. *Boys of Boise*. New York: Macmillan, 1966. Also New York: Crowell-Collier.

Menninger, Karl. *Man Against Himself*. New York: Harcourt, Brace & World, 1938.

Mitgang, Herbert. *The Man Who Rode the Tiger*. New York: Lippincott, 1963.

Moley, Raymond. *Tribunes of the People*. New Haven: Yale University Press, 1932.

Murtagh, John M., and Harris, Sara. *Cast the First Stone*. New York: McGraw-Hill, 1957.

Schur, Edwin M. *Crimes Without Victims*. Englewood Cliffs: Prentice-Hall, 1965.

Sutherland, Edwin H. *White Collar Crime*. New York: Holt, Rinehart and Winston, 1949, also 1961.

Tannenbaum, Frank. *Crime and the Community*. New York: Columbia University Press, 1938.

Thompson, Hunter S. *Hell's Angels*. New York: Random House, 1966. Also New York: Ballantine.

Weinberg, Arthur (ed.). *Attorney for the Damned*. New York: Simon & Schuster, 1957.

ARTICLES

Foote, Caleb. "Vagrancy-Type Law and Its Administration," *University of Pennsylvania Law Review*, Vol. 104, p. 603 (1956.)

Selected Bibliography

Mills, James. "The Detective," *Life*, December 3, 1965, p. 90D.

Packer, Herbert L. Review of "The Challenge of Crime in a Free Society," *New York Review of Books*, October 12, 1967, p. 17.

Schelling, Thomas C. "Economic Analysis and Organized Crime," in President's Commission on Law Enforcement and Administration of Justice, *Task Force Report: Organized Crime*, p. 114, Washington, D.C., U.S.G.P.O., 1967.

Taft, Donald R. "Influence of the General Culture on Crime," *Federal Probation*, Vol. 30, p. 16 (1966).

Wilmer, Harry A. "Good Guys and Bad Guys," *Federal Probation*, Vol. 30, p. 8 (1966).

REPORTS AND STUDIES

National Commission on Law Observance and Enforcement, *Report on Prohibition* (1931).

President's Commission on Law Enforcement and Administration of Justice, *The Challenge of Crime in a Free Society*, Washington, D.C., U.S.G.P.O., 1967.

Seabury, Samuel. *Final Report of Investigation of the Magistrate's Courts in the First Judicial Department* (N.Y.), March 28, 1932.

CASES

Fenster *v.* Leary, 20 N.Y.2d 309 (1967).

MISCELLANEOUS

FBI Press Release, January 6, 1966.

CHAPTER 3

BOOKS

Inbau, Fred E., and Reid, John E. *Criminal Interrogation and Confessions*. Williams & Wilkins: 1962 (revised ed. 1967).

LaFave, Wayne R. *Arrest*. Boston: Little, Brown, 1965.

Lowenthal, Max. *The Federal Bureau of Investigation*. New York: Sloane Associates, 1950.

Medalie, Richard J. *From Escobedo to Miranda*. Washington, D.C.: Lerner Law Book Co., 1966.

ARTICLES

Hoover, J. Edgar. "Civil Liberties and Law Enforcement: The Role of the FBI," *Iowa Law Review*, Vol. 37, p. 175 (1952).

"Playboy Panel: Crisis in Law Enforcement," *Playboy*, March 1966, p.47.

REPORTS AND STUDIES

American Law Institute, *Model Code of Pre-Arraignment Procedure*, Tentative Draft No. 1, March 1966.

National Commission on Law Observance and Enforcement, *Report on Lawlessness in Law Enforcement* (1931).
Report of the Attorney General's Committee on Poverty and the Administration of Criminal Justice, 1963 (Francis A. Allen, Chairman).
United States Commission on Civil Rights, *Law Enforcement, A Report on Equal Protection in the South*, Washington, D.C., U.S.G.P.O., 1965.

CASES

Escobedo *v.* Illinois, 378 U.S. 441 (1964).
Gideon *v.* Wainwright, 372 U.S. 335 (1963).
Mallory *v.* United States, 354 U.S. 449 (1957).
Miranda *v.* Arizona, 384 U.S. 436 (1966).
Watts *v.* Indiana, 338 U.S. 49 (1949).

MISCELLANEOUS

Hoover, J. Edgar, Letter to *Atlantic Monthly,* December, 1966, p. 46.
Omnibus Crime Bill for the District of Columbia, Public Law 90–226 (1967).
Proceedings of the Attorney General's Conference on Crime (1934).
Proceedings of National Conference on Bail and Criminal Justice, 1964, U.S. Department of Justice (1965).
United States Senate, Subcommittee on Criminal Law and Procedures of the Committee on the Judiciary, Hearings on [Various] Crime Bills, March 22–24 and May 10–11, 1966, 89th Congress, 2d Session.

CHAPTER 4

BOOKS

Bedford, Sybille. *The Trial of Dr. Adams.* New York: Simon & Schuster, 1958. Also New York: Grove Press, Inc.
Frank, Jerome. *Courts on Trial.* Princeton: Princeton University Press, 1949. Also New York: Atheneum.
Frankfurter, Felix. *The Case of Sacco and Vanzetti.* Boston: Little, Brown & Co., 1927. Also New York: Universal Library, 1962.
Golden, Harry. *A Little Girl Is Dead.* Cleveland: World, 1965. Also New York: Avon.
Kefauver, Estes. *Crime in America.* New York: Doubleday, 1951.
Kirchheimer, Otto. *Political Justice.* Princeton: Princeton University Press, 1961.
Lasswell, Harold. *Power and Personality.* New York: Norton, 1948. Also New York: Viking, 1962.
Moley, Raymond. *Politics and Criminal Prosecution.* New York: Minton, Balch & Co., 1929.
Schneir, Walter and Miriam. *Invitation to an Inquest.* New York: Doubleday, 1965. Also New York: Delta-Dell.
Williams, Edward Bennett. *One Man's Freedom.* New York: Atheneum, 1962. Also New York: Popular Library.

Selected Bibliography

ARTICLES

Darrow, Clarence. "Crime and the Alarmists," *Harper's*, Vol. 153, p. 535 (1926).
Douglas, William O. "The Public Trial and the Free Press," *American Bar Association Journal*, Vol. 46, p. 840 (1960).
Kaufman, Irving R. "The Apalachin Trial: Further Observations on Pre-Trial in Criminal Cases," *Journal of the American Judicature Society*, Vol. 44, p. 53 (1960).
Lewis, Anthony. "British Verdict on Trial-by-Press," *New York Times Magazine*, June 20, 1965, p. 14.
Mayer, Martin. " 'Hogan's Office' Is a Kind of Ministry of Justice," *New York Times Magazine*, July 23, 1967, p. 7.

REPORTS AND STUDIES

National Commission on Law Observance and Enforcement, *Report on Prosecution* (1931).
United States Senate, Third Interim Report of the Special Committee to Investigate Organized Crime in Interstate Commerce, Senate Report No. 307, 82d Congress, 1st Session (1951).

CASES

Berger *v.* United States, 295 U.S. 78 (1935).
Bufalino, United States *v.*, 285 F2d 408 (2d Cir. 1960).
Frank *v.* Mangum, 237 U.S. 309 (1915).
Kleinman, United States *v.*, 107 F. Supp. 407 (D.D.C. 1952).
Rosenberg, United States *v.*, 195 F2d 583, *cert. denied*, 344 U.S. 838 (1952).
Sacher *v.* United States, 343 U.S. 1 (1952).

CHAPTER 5

BOOKS

Bedford, Sybille. *The Trial of Dr. Adams.* New York: Simon & Schuster, 1958. Also New York: Grove Press, Inc.
Friendly, Alfred, and Goldfarb, Ronald. *Crime and Publicity.* New York: Twentieth Century Fund, 1967.
Lofton, John. *Justice and the Press.* Boston: Beacon Press, 1966.
Train, Arthur. *Courts, Criminals, and the Camorra.* New York: C. Scribner's Sons, 1911.

ARTICLES

Broeder, Dale. "Voir Dire Examinations: An Empirical Study," *Southern California Law Review*, Vol. 38, p. 503 (1965).
Kopkind, Andrew. "Times Square," *New York Review of Books*, May 4, 1967, p. 12.
Taylor, Telford. "Crime Reporting and Publicity of Criminal Proceedings," *Columbia Law Review*, Vol. 66, p. 34 (1966).

Selected Bibliography

Wessel, Milton. "Controlling Prejudicial Publicity in Criminal Trials," *Journal of American Judicature Society*, Vol. 48, p. 105 (1964).

REPORTS AND STUDIES

American Bar Association, *Standards Relating to Fair Trial and Free Press*, Tentative Draft, December 1966, Final Draft adopted by ABA, February 19, 1968.
American Newspaper Publishers Association, *Free Press and Fair Trial* (1967).
American Society of Newspaper Editors, *Report of Press-Bar Committee*, April 14, 1965.
Medina, Harold R., Chairman. *Freedom of the Press and Fair Trial.* Final Report by the Special Committee on Radio, Television, and the Administration of Justice of the Association of the Bar of the City of New York. New York: Columbia University Press, 1967.
Warren Commission, *Report of the President's Commission on the Assassination of President Kennedy*, Ch. 5 (1964).

CASES

Sheppard *v.* Maxwell, 384 U.S. 333 (1966). For District Court opinion in same case, see 231 F. Supp. 37 (S.D. Ohio 1964).
Stroble *v.* California, 343 U.S. 181 (1952).
Van Duyne, State *v.*, 43 N.J. 369 (1964).

MISCELLANEOUS

Katzenbach, Nicholas DeB., Attorney General. Statement of Policy Concerning the Release of Information by Personnel of the Department of Justice Relating to Criminal Proceedings, 28 CFR § 50.2 (1965).

CHAPTER 6

BOOKS

Dash, Samuel, Knowlton, Robert, and Schwartz, Richard. *The Eavesdroppers.* New Brunswick, N. J.: Rutgers University Press, 1959.
Kennedy, Robert F. *The Enemy Within.* New York: Harper & Brothers, 1960. Also New York: Popular Library.
Lowenthal, Max. *The Federal Bureau of Investigation.* New York: Sloane Associates, 1950.
Mollenhoff, Clark. *Tentacles of Power: The Story of Jimmy Hoffa.* Cleveland: World, 1965.
Murtagh, John M., and Harris, Sara. *Cast the First Stone.* New York: McGraw-Hill, 1957.

ARTICLES

Donnelly, Richard. "Judicial Control of Informants, Spies, Stool Pigeons, and Agents Provocateurs," *Yale Law Journal*, Vol. 60, p. 1091 (1951).

Goldstein, Joseph. "Police Discretion Not To Invoke the Criminal Process: Low-Visibility Decisions in the Administration of Justice," *Yale Law Journal*, Vol. 69, p. 543 (1960).

Jackson, Bruce. "Exiles from the American Dream—'The Junkie and the Cop,'" *The Atlantic Monthly*, Vol. 219, p. 44 (1967).

Partin, Edward. "An Insider's Chilling Story of Hoffa's Savage Kingdom," *Life*, May 15, 1964.

Suydam, Henry. "Hoffa: How They Nailed Him," *Life*, March 13, 1964.

Turner, William. "I Was a Burglar, Wiretapper, Bugger, and Spy for the F.B.I.," *Ramparts*, November, 1966, p. 51.

CASES

Berger v. New York, 388 U.S. 41 (1967).

Dardi, United States v., 330 F.2d 316 (2d Cir.), *cert. denied*, 379 U.S. 845 (1964).

Dennis, United States v., 341 U.S. 494 (1950).

Hoffa v. United States, 385 U.S. 293 (1966).

Katz, United States v., — U.S. — (1967).

Lewis v. United States, 385 U.S. 206 (1966).

McCray v. Illinois, 386 U.S. 300 (1967).

Massiah v. United States, 377 U.S. 201 (1964).

Mesarosh v. United States, 352 U.S. 1 (1956).

Nickens v. United States, 323 F.2d 808 (D.C. Cir. 1963).

Olmstead v. United States, 277 U.S. 438 (1928).

On Lee, United States v., 343 U.S. 747 (1952).

Osborn v. United States, 385 U.S. 323 (1966).

Rosenberg, United States v., 195 F.2d 583 (2d Cir.), *cert. denied*, 344 U.S. 838 (1952).

Sorrells v. United States, 287 U.S. 435 (1932).

MISCELLANEOUS

FBI Press Release, January 6, 1966.

CHAPTER 7

BOOKS

Frank, Jerome. *Courts on Trial*, Princeton: Princeton University Press, 1949. Also New York: Atheneum.

Jones, Harry (ed.). *The Courts, the Public, and the Law Explosion*, Englewood Cliffs: Prentice-Hall, 1965.

ARTICLES

Dash, Samuel. "Cracks in the Foundation of Criminal Justice," *Northwestern University Law Review*, Vol. 46, p. 385 (1951).

Downie, Leonard. Series of articles on the Court of General Sessions, Washington *Post*, 1965–1966.
Hoagland, Jim. " 'Revolutionary' Judge on the General Sessions Bench, Potomac" (Washington *Post*, September 25, 1966, p. 7).

REPORTS AND STUDIES

President's Commission on Law Enforcement and Administration of Justice, *The Challenge of Crime in a Free Society*, Chs. 5 and 9, Washington, D.C., U.S.G.P.O., 1967.
Shadoan, George. *Criminal Justice in the Court of General Sessions* (Georgetown University Law Center, unpublished manuscript, 1961).
Subin, Harry I. *Criminal Justice in a Metropolitan Court*, U.S. Department of Justice, 1966.

CASES

Driver *v.* Hannant, 356 F.2d 761 (4th Cir. 1966).
Easter *v.* District of Columbia, 361 F.2d 50 (D.C. Cir. 1966).
Ricks, District of Columbia *v.*, Crim. Action No. D.C. 3050–66, June 16, 1966.

CHAPTER 8

BOOKS

Allen, Francis A. *The Borderland of Criminal Justice.* Chicago: The University of Chicago Press, 1964.
Darrow, Clarence. *Crime—Its Cause and Treatment.* New York: Thomas Y. Crowell, 1922.
Hall, Jerome. *Theft, Law and Society* (2d ed.). Indianapolis: Bobbs-Merrill Co., 1952.
Martin, John Bartlow. *Break Down the Walls.* London: Gollancz, 1955.
Newman, Donald J. *Conviction: The Determination of Guilt or Innocence Without Trial.* Boston: Little, Brown Co., 1967.
Shaw, George Bernard. *The Crime of Imprisonment.* New York: The Citadel Press, 1961 (paperback).
Sykes, Gresham. *Society of Captives.* Princeton: Princeton University Press, 1958. Also New York: Atheneum.

ARTICLES

Bennett, James T. "Our Penal System," *American Criminal Law Quarterly*, Vol. 4, p. 68 (1966).
Carpenter, Lawrence A. "The Federal Work Release Program," *Nebraska Law Review*, Vol. 45, p. 690 (1966).
Darrow, Clarence. "Crime and the Alarmists," *Harper's*, Vol. 153, p. 535 (1926).

Selected Bibliography

Gough, Aidan R. "The Expungement of Adjudication Records of Juvenile and Adult Offenders: A Problem of Status," *Washington University Law Quarterly*, Vol. 1966, p. 147 (1966).

Hamblin, Dora Jane. "Her Honor Bops the Hoodlums," *Life*, July 9, 1965, p. 74.

Harper's, Special Supplement on Crime and Punishment, April, 1964.

REPORTS AND STUDIES

American Bar Association, *Standards Relating to Appellate Review of Sentences*, Tentative Draft, April, 1967, adopted with modifications by ABA, February 19, 1968.

American Law Institute, *Model Penal Code* (Proposed Official Draft, 1962).

Chicago Crime Commission, *Bulletins* (1919–1933).

Joint Commission on Mental Illness and Health, *Action for Mental Health*. New York: Basic Books, 1961.

President's Commission on Law Enforcement and Administration of Justice, *The Challenge of Crime in a Free Society*. Chs. 3, 5, and 6, Washington, D.C., U.S.G.P.O., 1967.

President's Commission on Law Enforcement and Administration of Justice, *Task Force Reports: Corrections, The Courts*, Ch. 2, Washington, D.C., U.S.G.P.O., 1967.

Report of the President's Commission on Crime in the District of Columbia, Ch. 10, Washington, D.C., U.S.G.P.O., 1966.

MISCELLANEOUS

Clark, Ramsey, Attorney General. Address to Washington Citizens Council of National Council on Crime and Delinquency, July 10, 1967.

Hoover, J. Edgar. Message from the Director, FBI Law Enforcement Bulletin, March, 1967.

Omnibus Crime Bill for the District of Columbia, Public Law 90–226 (1967).

CHAPTER 9

BOOKS

Arens, Richard, and Lasswell, Harold D. *In Defense of Public Order: The Emerging Field of Sanction Law*. New York: Columbia University Press, 1961.

Belli, Melvin. *Dallas Justice*. New York: David McKay Co., 1964.

Bok, Curtis. *Star Wormwood*. New York: Knopf, 1959. Also New York: Signet.

Darrow, Clarence. *The Story of My Life.* New York: Scribner's, 1934.
Feifer, George. *Justice in Moscow.* New York: Simon & Schuster, 1964. Also New York: Delta-Dell.
Frank, Jerome. *Courts on Trial.* Princeton: Princeton University Press, 1949. Also New York: Atheneum.
Kaplan, John K., and Waltz, Jon R. *The Trial of Jack Ruby.* New York: Macmillan, 1965.
Kennedy, Robert F. *The Pursuit of Justice,* Ch. 10. New York: Harper & Row, 1964.
Lasswell, Harold D. *Power and Personality.* New York: Norton, 1948. Also New York: Viking.
Lewis, Anthony. *Gideon's Trumpet.* New York: Random House, 1964. Also New York: Vintage.
Pound, Roscoe. *Criminal Justice in America.* New York: Henry Holt & Co., 1930.
Szasz, Thomas S. *Law, Liberty and Psychiatry.* New York: Macmillan, 1963.

ARTICLES

Bedford, Sybille. "Violence, Froth, Sob Stuff—Was Justice Done?" *Life,* March 27, 1964, p. 32.
Curtis, Charles P. "Ethics in the Law," *Stanford Law Review,* Vol. 4, p. 477 (1952).
Kadish, Sanford. "The Advocate and the Expert—Counsel in the Peno-Correctional Process," *Minnesota Law Review,* Vol. 45, p. 803 (1961).
Pye, A. Kenneth. "The Legal Needs of the Poor," *Columbia Law Review,* Vol. 66, p. 286 (1966).
Rostow, Eugene. "The Warren Report—The Legacy of Grief," *Yale Law Report,* Winter 1965, p. 1.
Smith, Marshall. "His Lifetime Record—Won: 700, Lost: 1," *Life,* April 1, 1966, p. 92.

REPORTS AND STUDIES

President's Commission on Law Enforcement and the Administration of Justice, *Task Force Report: The Courts,* Ch. 2, Washington, D.C., U.S.G.P.O., 1967.
Report of the Attorney General's Committee on Poverty and the Administration of Criminal Justice, 1963 (Francis A. Allen, Chairman).
Report of the Joint Conference on Professional Responsibility of the Association of American Law Schools and the American Bar Association (1958).
Warren Commission, *Report of the President's Commission on the Assassination of President Kennedy* (1964).

CASES

Bergen *v.* United States, 295 U.S. 78 (1935).
Gault *v.* Arizona, 387 U.S. 1 (1967).
Gideon *v.* Wainwright, 372 U.S. 335 (1963).

Index

INDEX

Ethics of advocacy, 76, 180, 181, 182

Fear of Crime, 9–10, 26–27, 67–69, 167–68
Federal Bureau of Investigation (FBI), 4, 5, 7, 21, 47, 48, 62, 63–66, 86, 111, 112, 119, 156; FBI informants, 117
Fenster case, 34
Fifth Amendment, *see* Self-incrimination
Finch, Stanley, 112
First Amendment, *see* Contempt power
Foote, Caleb, 33
Foreman, Percy, 178, 185
Fortas, Abe, 69, 179, 184, 186, 187, 189, 190
"Four-time loser" in N.Y., 156–57
Frank, Jerome, 75, 144, 181
Frankfurter, Felix, x, 84, 92, 127
Friendly, Alfred, 103
Fulbright, J. William, x

Garrison, Jim, 73
Gault case, 187–89
Gaynor, William, 38
Gideon case, 50, 59, 141, 173, 179–80, 183–84
Gideon, Clarence, history of, 185–88
Gideon's Trumpet (Lewis), 173
Golden, Harry, 42, 82
Goldwater, Barry, 13–14, 51, 67
Goodwin, Richard, 15
Government funds for assigned counsel, 145
Graham, Fred, 19, 22
Greene, Harold A., 144–45, 146
Greenglass, David, 117
Guterma, Alexander, 118

Harlan, John M., 60, 65, 67
Harris, Sara, 37
Harvard Law School, 184
Hell's Angels gang, 25, 26
Hiss, Alger, 86

Hoffa, Jimmy, 119–25, 126, 127; jury-fixing case of, 75, 116, 120, 123, 124–25
Hogan, Frank, 87–88, 156
Holmes, Oliver W., 82–83, 89
Homosexuality, 36, 42–43, 44
Hoover, Herbert, 12
Hoover, J. Edgar, 4, 8, 11, 28, 43, 47, 48, 62–63, 111, 154–55

Immunity, granting of, to informers, 116
Imprisonment, scars of, 152
Inbau, Fred, 54–56, 130
Informers, 112–27; in narcotics cases, 115–16; granting immunity to, 116
Interracial crime, 9, 138
Interrogation, 45–70

Jackson, Robert H., 59
Jenkins, Walter, 43
Johnson, Lyndon, 3, 14, 21, 43, 51, 67, 144, 157
Jones, Harry, 144
Judges, in General Sessions Court, 137, 143, 144, 145
Judges' Rules, English, 61
Jury system, 73–74, 94, 97–98, 101
Justice Department, 27, 50, 120, 124, 125, 132, 133, 145, 156
Juvenile Court, 160, 188–89, 190
Juvenile reformatories, 186, 188

Katzenbach, Nicholas, 9, 57, 133, 141
Kaufman, Irving R., 80, 84–86, 161
Kefauver, Estes, 78–79
Kennedy, John F., 93
Kennedy, Robert, 119–23, 173, 183
Kopkind, Andrew, 107
Kross, Anna M., 38, 40

Lasswell, Harold, 179
"Lawlessness in Law Enforcement," Wickersham report on, 56–57

INDEX

About the Author

Robert M. Cipes was born in 1930 in Mount Vernon, N.Y., and received degrees from Harvard College and the Yale Law School. He is a former federal prosecutor and author of a highly acclaimed treatise on criminal procedure, published in 1965. He became interested in criminal law while working for the New Haven Public Defender and headed the Yale Law School Public Defenders. After graduation Mr. Cipes served as confidential law assistant to New York's highest court and then engaged in private practice in New York City before joining the Department of Justice. He has been a consultant to the Neighborhood Legal Services project in Washington and to the President's Commission on Crime in the District of Columbia. From 1966–67 he was Senior Research Attorney at the Georgetown University Institute of Criminal Law and Procedure, and in the 1968 spring term taught criminal law to undergraduates at the University of California in Santa Barbara. He now resides in the New York suburbs with his wife and three children. His articles on criminal law have appeared in *The Atlantic Monthly* and *The New Republic*.